Esoteric Publishing without the Corporate Control

Khem Publishing

Print ISBN: 9798281583268

Introduction:

It is with great joy that this book is released. What was possibly intended as a full exposition of Deon, or Semelas, within the Frères d'Orient, has—somewhere along the course of its production—taken a turn toward a different destination.

Having been exposed to nearly every major esoteric current, this text bears strong and nearly undeniable markers of the hand of Lewis S. Keizer.

How this material was kept from even his most prolific and well-researched bishop-scholar, Christine Payne-Towler—or from myself, as a member of his lost school of initiation—is a mystery. Nonetheless, following the visualizations (which seem to reveal an unimaginably hidden dimension of the tradition), the text shifts. The practical material disappears, and what follows are lectures—more cerebral, less embodied.

This is, of course, only my first impression—and it could be wrong. It seems that Keizer's scholarship asserts itself here in an unfamiliar, perhaps unrefined, way. And yet, the thought-forms remain present throughout the work.

With these prefatory remarks in place, it must be said: the book still holds tremendous merit. It offers insights and distinctions that have not been widely available.

The dream of an organization that syncretizes the traditions brought into it is strongly felt in these pages. That said, the excessive use of the term Templar presents a challenge, and the presence of the Grail motif suggests a later origin—likely during the Grail and Templar renaissance of the 1990s, or possibly earlier. In this sense, the work appears to be a forgotten relic of Keizer's thought—drifting between epochs, yet still vital.

These kinds of organizations often borrow teachings to build themselves into summa theologica-style bodies of instruction. Either Keizer was directly involved, or the original order that produced these documents used "Deon" as a pseudonym—possibly for an inner school of Keizer. This mirrors what we see in the ICES materials of Martinism, where a shift appears from the Richard Duc de Palatine corpus into a kind of "New Church," likely another Keizer production.

I don't feel remiss in revealing these details, as he has long since lost interest in matters of esotericism. Likely, due to the prolific nature of his output, there was a kind of burnout. A biblical scholar and deeply read researcher in his own right, Keizer's voice nonetheless echoes throughout this material.

The heavy reliance on idioms uniquely his—especially those rooted in his critique of Schweitzer's claims about the historical Jesus—are unmistakable. His insistence on the use of Yeshua, for instance, is strongly present. Still, despite these markers, the text is beautifully written and deserves serious consideration by those engaged in esoteric study.

I don't wish to bore the reader—or to fill this introduction with an excessive cataloging of Keizer's academic topoi—but it must be said: there are aspects of the tradition that could genuinely benefit from the insights offered here.

That said, it could just as well be that Deon was in fact the original author, and that this material reveals a hidden understanding within the order he was part of. Or perhaps the reverse is true: that Keizer lifted his foundational philosophy from Deon, and that this is the hidden root of what became his Temple of the Holy Grail in its pre-formation.

Another possibility is that the material is a hybrid—part Keizer, part Deon—and that Keizer revised or reworked the original text. Whatever the case may be, it's clear that the work carries genuine mystical significance, whether syncretic, original, or a synthesis of both traditions.

Getting this structural analysis out of the way, we can now turn to the true beauty of the work, and why it felt so important to bring it into book form.

At its heart, this text offers a renewed vision of the Order of Melchizedek—not simply as a priesthood, but as a neutral path that embraces both solar and lunar aspects of the divine. My hope for the material is simple and perhaps even naïve: that it may help restore balance to the force, to borrow a phrase from the Star Wars mythos. That is to say, to reintroduce a harmony between dualities often kept apart—male and female, light and dark, head and heart.

The chants, for instance, seem aligned with the Baal Shem Tov's approach to sacred utterance, and also bear a striking resemblance to the Rose-Croix d'Orient's use of the secret names of Metatron (a selection of which has been added in the appendix). Through a combination of vocalization and visualization, the work invites a state of spiritual resonance rather than mere intellectual understanding.

Some of the more imaginative claims—for instance, that Abraham and Sarah were the original "Templars" (though I prefer terms like Operator, Coën, or Emulator)—fall outside traditional esoteric teaching, yet they offer a mythic reframe that opens new symbolic horizons. The emphasis on the "Dark Mother" is also a powerful corrective, a gesture toward a more integrated spiritual view—one that balances the classic Father-Son-Spirit trinity with the Mother-Maiden-Crone triad, echoing the ancient cult of Kybele.

I personally found the visualization work to be one of the most resonant aspects of the book. Coupled with mantra and vocal work, it becomes a kind of esoteric syntax—a logic of energy, expressed through spontaneous inner images and the sounds that give them form.

Yes, some of the material is admittedly tedious in places—an occupational hazard of most channeled or highly symbolic works—but it offers moments of real luminosity. To counter this confusion Part I includes Semelas or Deon's 7 part study on Initiation. This should contextualize his particular meanings and definately give a broader view of the Initiatic Tradition, which some have even called the Primordial Church associated to the

3

antedilluvian mythos and stories

A personal favorite is the reimagining of the archangel Michael—not as a singular celestial being, but as a collective entity, evoking the vision of Ezekiel's chariot. This resonates not only with Hekhalot literature but also with the "Work of the Chariot" as framed by Maimonides, and later by Abulafia. These allusions suggest an awareness of the deeper mystical traditions of the Merkavah, perhaps hidden in plain sight.

The layers of Kabbalistic cosmology—Atziluth, Beriah, Yetzirah, Assiah—are not simply abstracted; they are made experiential through the visualizations, which makes the text all the more potent. The theory supports the imagery, and the imagery reinforces the theory. This interplay, more than anything, is what makes the book worth serious attention.

Originally I thought this was a sort of secret club of academics that studied the material and then synthesized all the phenomenology of the traditions encountered in a grand synthesis, naive, sure, but very indicative of the Christian Rosenkreutz movement and the erudition of the first Rosicrucians as well. Perhaps it would be a great time indeed, to learn how to harmonize our knowledge, ideologies, and identities. To learn the common brotherhood/sisterhood and move away from archaic forms of us vs. them, and me vs. you. Naive again, sure but with these kind of materials, perhaps the love of humanity will shine again in a few hearts, and we can approach the alter of our minds and consciousness with more fire than ever before, and the incense will reach the emperean , finally.

On Initiation

(This series of 8 Speeches forms part of the 34 Speeches that Demetrius Se-melas made on Alchemy in the Lodge of the Essenes of the Order of the Martinists, in Cairo, 1911.)

First Speech by D. Semelas

The State of an **Initiate**

(19 /10 /1911. Cairo, Egypt)

The purpose of our studies on Initiation in general is to give our brothers and sisters an accurate idea of the work that we propose to carry out in the future. In this manner, through their study, they will be able to find the path that is proper to each personally, the one which each is called to follow.

This study will clearly show you the Unity of the Tradition that has come to us, either through direct transmission or through revelation.

Traditionally, there are 7 degrees in Initiation. Sometimes these are summed up to 3, and sometimes to 2.

The presentation in 3 degrees teaches the mysteries and gives the keys to the 3 planes, the physical, the astral, and the mental. These are analysed: in the science of the physical plane or Alche-my, in the science of the psychical plane or Astrosophy – Astron-omy according to the time and place, and finally in the science of the mental plane or Theurgy.

Each of these 3 divisions comprises both theory and practice.

The division into 7 degrees is presented as 4 divisions for the-ory and 3 divisions for practice. These 7 divisions were illustrat-ed by the 7 steps of the Temple of Eternal Wisdom, as Kunrath presented them.

In locations where traditional Initiation was given, nobody was permitted to aim at the 5th or 7th degree before having climbed the first ones.

The Initiator assessed his Initiate's progress by observing its effects on him, and imposed what we call trials on his disciple.

5

These trials varied according to the School, but they all had the same aim. We shall speak about this further on.

Here are the 7 traditional divisions of the Great Initiation:

1st part (theory)	1st degree:	Mystery of the Unity
(Unitary and	2nd degree:	Mystery of the Binary
Traditional	3rd degree:	Mystery of the Quaternary
Principle)	4th degree:	Mystery of the Ternary
2nd part	5th or 1st degree:	Adaptation of knowledge &
(practical)		practical realizations, all of which lead to the mastery of the physical plane or to the mastery of Alchemy. (adaptation and 6th or 2nd degree: Mastery of the Astral or the psychical plane.
realization)	7th or 3rd degree:	Adaptation in the mental plane or Theurgy.

As you see, it would be foolish to wish to follow the path of Initiation starting from the end. Some imprudent and ignorant amateurs did so, and the result was exactly the opposite of what they sought. Since the Invisible did not respond to their desires, they were unable to bring about any effectuation. Some of them whose character was weak, were frustrated, fell into the nihilism of atheism, and lost faith in Initiatic work and study. It is due to this thoughtlessness and this erroneous estimate, to this impatience to effectuate something, and to this foolish untested self-confidence that they were defeated and ended up unsuccessful and disillusioned. At the start, they were certainly full of good intentions, but by not following the path from its very beginning, they opened the door wide to scepticism, and finally lost their peace of mind.

I intend to provide each of you with the maximum means, and this is why we shall start on the principles and work our way progressively. We shall go through the first 4 degrees quite rapidly, which each of you will develop according to your aptitude, and then proceed to the particular study of the 3 branches of practice.

*
* *

Let us take one of the three branches of the practical part at random, for example, mastery over the astral plane. We observe that in this branch, just as in the other two, all the work requires the possession of certain qualities and virtues and the realization of a certain state.

In fact, anyone who desires to approach the sanctuary and become master of some practice must try as much as possible to give birth to certain virtues within him/her. These are virtues that he does not possess. They have been designated to him through the teachings that he received. He must then cultivate them to the utmost and make them bear fruit, otherwise he runs the risk of being forever excluded from all initiatic practice or, if he attempts the practice, he then runs the risk of ending up in failures and their subsequent evils.

Therefore the disciple must:
1) Be morally pure. This means that through willpower, he must manage to overcome his passions and vices, banish hate from his soul, as well as everything that can hinder him from doing his humanitarian duties. Because most of his imperfections are the product of the soul, they must be fought in their own domain. And it is only by means of his Will that Man can get rid of them.
2) Have faith. He must believe in the existence of these 3 planes and firmly want to act on them.
3) Ignore fear. However, he must bear in mind the importance of the danger that exists. One can attain no mastery whatever if one is afraid.

One who is not pure of heart, one who is thwarted by hate, one who is feeble of will and lacks faith, one who is afraid of his very shadow, who is afraid of the darkness of the unknown must retrace his steps and leave the path. He cannot seek to acquire knowledge of the great mysteries.

When seen from a distance, all these great mysteries correspond to something that is beautiful and brilliant. When they are approached, reality is then seen as

7

monstrous. Indeed take, for example, a person who externally appears beautiful and agreeable to you. What is this person like internally? What is his soul like? It may be full of passions and weaknesses. The psychical, the astral, the plane of the soul is full of all human exhalations. The astral is ugly, and it is in order to prevent you from getting disillusioned that I exhort you, my dear brothers and sisters, to study yourselves, to purify yourselves and to examine your conscience and your heart.

In ancient times anyone who demanded Initiation was compelled to undergo very hard trials. These were not meant to test his physical prowess but to assess his courage. The Masters Initiators chose as their disciples only persons who showed courage in the face of danger and those possessing great knowledge. This was because of the importance of Initiation and because of the active role of Man on the physical and astral planes. It was also because they feared disastrous and regrettable consequences that were likely to result if the one who experimented was ignorant or cowardly. In our days, such trials are no longer applied, and it is now up to the one who desires Initiation to purify his imperfect being through willpower.

Brethren, what did I tell you at the time of your Initiation? I spoke to you of the Unity presented symbolically to you by the 3 luminaries that represent the unity of Initiation on the 3 planes. In our talks on Alchemy, I explained to you the Unity in the physical plane. I shall now explain to you the Unity in the astral or psychical plane. Just as you see 3 flames springing from 3 different luminaries and forming one and unique light, so too, from the united souls of three or more persons there springs a single psychical radiation.

You know the constitution of the human body. Let us now see how the astral or psychical plane or the soul is constituted. The soul or astral is the product of the Essential Force acting on Matter. Matter is thus spiritualized and its etherization or sublimation is the result of the action of the energy of the Spirit on it. This soul, this astral, this psyche is an existing life and possibly verifiable by our animic senses, for it issues from the body and radiates. Because it is the outcome of the union of the 2 Principles of the Binary – Force or Spirit, and Matter – the soul is a third and factitious life.

Let us now see why the soul or astral is produced and what its purpose is. In Creation, all beings are united with one another by means of a mediator. This mediator is invisible to the human eye, but is existence is continuously demonstrated by the experience and the actions in everyday life. It is needless to enumerate to you the proofs of the existence of the soul. The soul, the astral, governs all, encompasses all, and impregnates all. On our Earth it influences the mineral, vegetal and animal kingdoms. In the Universe it regulates the movement of the worlds and unites them for, since the void does not exist, it is filled with Matter that is etherized to a smaller of greater degree. As a consequence, the purpose of the creation of the soul is to effectuate the 1st Natural Law, the occult union of all created beings with one another, as also their collective union with the Creator.

The whole of Man's life is dependent on the soul. Even before Man's birth, the Spirit fashions the embryo by means of the astral. After Man's birth the Spirit devotes all its attention and efforts so as to form a healthy body. It seeks to acquire a beautiful covering (envelope) by means of which it (the Spirit) can learn to work on the physical plane. There are persons who managed to reach a superior state of being and from there on sought to penetrate higher than the physical plane by developing their soul and their spirit, which is covered by the soul. They were able to live in half of this Invisible plane and later in the whole of it.

What theory could we give so as to explain the creation of the psychic fluid or astral? A substance can become etherized only if two states that are contrary to one another adapt themselves so as to form a third, which is a factitious, a false state. These two initial states are Matter and Spirit, which are represented in Masonic symbolism by the two pillars of the Temple, one of which is black and the other is white, one is square and the other is round. This indicates two contrary things and this symbolism of the two pillars explains to you the great law according to which a third agent can result from two agents that are negative as regards each other. In this case the result is the Astral. You can find a corresponding action in Alchemy, as well as in the other branches, for the Law of Unity is the same law in all the branches of Initiation.

The symbol of what manifests Truth is at one and the same time a reality, but there also exist adaptations and emblems on all the planes, in all areas and in all the branches of Initiation. In truth the life of Christ can be adapted to everything. An apostle of the Light and of Truth cannot have a life that is not in accord with the Law that governs Creation. Since he is universal, he must accordingly render the data of the Universal Law a reality.

The two pillars designate two states that are contrary to one another and express the binary that we can find everywhere present.
*
* *

The astral, the soul, the psychical plane, which is the product of

9

Matter and Spirit, is neither Matter nor Spirit. It is simply a mediator. Do not seek to find spirituality, intelligence or reason in it. It will deceive you, and all those who have consulted it and asked its opinion – one that it cannot give – ended up with sad results. Still, the Initiate must seek to find out what is behind the physical plane and get to know the astral.

Within the material plane you cannot find any virtue whatever that is superior to instinct. The astral, the soul – which is the etherization of the physical – possesses all the imperfections of the physical and is distinguished by its great incoherence. It can only serve as a mediator so as to enable one to see and control what is more difficult to perceive through physical sight.

By evocations, ceremonials and practices, the Initiate obtains mastery over the astral, while still remaining on the physical plane. As regards what is called 'voyage to the astral', it is considered as exceptional as the condensations of a psychical nature (those of psychurgy). One who is called to such effectuations will eventually know how to find the requisite means and the necessary superior assistance to do so.

On the **Quaternary**

(26 /10 /1911. Cairo, Egypt)

In our study of the initiatic theory we examined the Unity and the Binary. Today we shall study the Quaternary. The astral proper resides in the Unity, that is to say, in the mixed (com-pound) basis of the Universal All. In the Binary there is an agent and a patient – two equal contraries. The Ternary be-longs to the mental plane in particular but we shall not deal with it for the present. Today we shall examine the force of the Quaternary in both the physical and the astral planes.

But let us first see its composition. Two contrary principles form the Binary; the force that balances them brings them to the Ter-nary; the product of the two balanced principles contributes to form the Quaternary.

You have probably not grasped very well what I have just told you. The basis of all Initiations is found in the theories that I am now presenting to you. But I shall be as explicit as possible so that you may understand this better.

The importance of the Quaternary in the astral provides most useful knowledge to one who desires to attain mastery over this plane. As we previously demonstrated, in the physical plane the occult force is derived from the union of two contrary physical principles. In like manner, the astral plane is produced from two contrary principles. Here is an example: On the physical plane, man as such is considered positive whereas woman is considered negative. The attraction of these two principles produces a force, which is sexual love; this in turn produces a neutral being, the offspring…..and thus the Quaternary is formed.

The same analysis can be made as regards the astral. The necessi-ty of the existence of two principles is everywhere present. For example, would good exist if we did not have the notion of evil? Would we have the perception of daylight if night did not exist? No, we would not. Human thought would not have any concept of all these. Every realization requires the contribution of two contrary agents. Therefore, in the astral there exist two princi-ples, two forces, two contrary fluids, whose union   brings about equilibrium.

We previously defined the astral as vivified and vivifying etheric

11

Substance, which acts on Matter and etherizes it, giving it a factitious life. This force acts on everything in Nature and produces and etherification, and its action differs according to the gender, kind, etc, of the 'patients'. When this force acts on mineral Matter it produces electricity, which is a mixture of Matter and of the Force that vivifies Matter. Recent discoveries have proved that electricity contains Matter – in very small quantities it is true – but its presence is enough to prove the material origin of electricity. The product of what the Spiritual Force produced, by acting on mineral Matter, is the mineral astral agent, whose active principle is the Force and whose passive principle is Matter. The action of the Cosmic Force on planets creates this mediator, this general agent, this intermediary fluid that unites asterisms to one another.

Since we see a mineral astral, there must also be an astral of the vegetal kingdom. This one differs greatly from the former. The mineral astral produces a kind of fire that supports Matter. The vegetal astral generates a vivifying production which is of service to the animal kingdom and makes it live. It is a kind of fluid that is susceptible to take on a vegetal form.

As such, the astral composition of the mineral kingdom does not possess any definite form. Electricity cannot be seen or discerned through our material eyes. Though what we see as a spark is visible, it still does not take on a particular form. On the other hand, the vegetal astral presents its form to its material principle. One who is able to see well, can see in the neighbourhood of forests other forests superimposed on the lateral ones. In general, the astral of a vegetal can be seen by the imprint of form that it has made on its original patient (substance).

In the animal astral, the form is imprinted, and this creates a factitious life, which becomes adapted and remains latent in an astral state. It is felt in both the animal kingdom and in Man. Some sensitive persons have seen in the astral level various animals of strange and bizarre forms that eventually disappeared. These beings are nonentities; they are animal astral imprints that are destined to eventually dissolve after their formation.

Bear in mind that the astral is not born as a result of an act of Will. In all three kingdoms – mineral, vegetal and animal – as well as in Man, it is the result of the association of Matter and Spiritual Force. Man does not create his astral. His Will has no part whatever in this. Every union produces a result; everything proves this to be so and Science has the same opinion on the subject. The Spiritual Principle Force on the one hand, and Matter, which is another fundamental Principle of Creation on the other, produce the balance of harmony or neutrality, which binds one to the other.

Otherwise life could not exist and be manifest, and Matter would be dead.

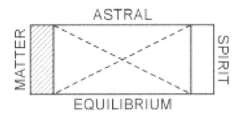

Here is the schema of the realization of the Quaternary when applied to the astral. Among the general symbols that we constantly see, and by a new application to what we are studying, the two pillars of the Temple represent the two principles, the black one represents Matter and the white one represents the Spiritual Force. But a common support is needed for these pillars to remain upright, to be located in a particular place. This support will thus provide them with a plane of action, will unite them so that they may contribute to attain a definite purpose. This support is equilibrium, represented here by the line of the earth, on which the two pillars rest. Thus balanced, the pillars unite for a common task. Their union serves to sustain what is placed on top of them. The action of the Spiritual Force on Matter brings forth the astral, Life, which is the product of this reaction, animating Matter and making it grow.

In this manner we have this schema of the astral Quaternary – the two Principles, Matter and Spirit, which are balanced and thus produce the Astral.

Let us sum up in order to better grasp the whole meaning. We know what the positive is; it is a Force, the Spirit. The negative is Matter. The result is the Astral and Equilibrium. It is the link, the receptacle in or on which the action takes place. In Creation, it is the Universal All, where the work of Nature takes place, the quaternary work. It stands to reason that if we wish to form a chemical or other compound, we need a receptacle; if we wish to construct a temple, we need the ground on which the pillars will stand. It is only this agent, Equilibrium, that permits the action of Force on Matter, and this mystery is one of the most incomprehensible.

The ancient Greeks conceived an allegory so as to put a check on the curiosity of the profane (secular), for the Initiates knew what it was all about. It was the myth of Atlas bearing the world on his shoulders. The matter was considered to be quite a

13

clear description, since nobody would think of wondering on what Atlas himself was supported! So you see that we always come back to the subject of Equilibrium.

The Earth, just like every other star, rests on or in the bosom of a non-material agent, which continually demonstrates its presence. You will object by saying that the equilibrium of the worlds is due to the attraction and repulsion of the stars on one another. This is very true, but this attraction and this repulsion must also be expressed in some place, in some kind of substance. And since everything has a beginning and an end, at a certain point the stars cease to exist. On what then are these stars at the very edge supported? What encompasses them? Again we come back to Equilibrium and we are obliged to admit its very important role.

Now that we have understood what the Quaternary is, we can more easily form a general idea of the usefulness of the occult theory. Both the creator and the created exist in the astral quaternary. The creator comprises Force, Matter, and Equilibrium. The created is the result of the concurrence of these three. It is the Astral.

Let us now see if, by analogy, the quaternary exists on another plane, on the physical, for example. The four material principles that make up this plane are the four elements. As you learnt in the Course on Alchemy, this composition of the four elements is created as well as creative Matter. From now on you can see the analogy between the two planes, the physical and the astral. The law of this analogy was defined by Hermes Trismegistus in a great symbolic manner: *"What is above is like what is below, and what is below is like what is above"*. The Hindus have the same dogma, expressed in a different manner: *"What is in the large is like what is in the small, and what is in the small is like what is in the large"*.

What is the usefulness of the quaternary in the study of the Astral? It is quite clear that, since the Astral is a creative and created agent, a person who can have a concept of it and discern the general direction of this creation can penetrate into it and direct it according to their will. Therefore it is by means of a total knowledge of the quaternary that this result can be attained.

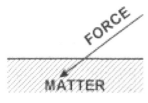

I shall now give you a tangible explanation, a general outline of the way in which the Astral is accomplished. Matter is something passive into which Force is thrust. In other terms, the action of the Spirit involuted in Matter, gives us the following diagram. The horizontal line represents the extremity of Matter, which is here depicted by the darkened area. The descending slanted line expresses the Spiritual Force. The action of this Force on Matter provokes numerous physical states, such as heat, fire, dissolution, etc. These states differ in degree and variety, depending on Matter.

Here you can see a sketch of the formation of the astral. Let us imagine a mass of Matter. As the arrow penetrates into it in a slanting direction and as it involutes into Matter and begins to act within it, it first produces very intense heat. This is schematically located on the line a-a. The continuous action of the Force then

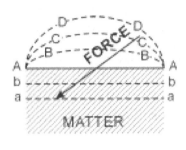

produces a second state in which the heat is less intense but more dense. In the diagram this is located in the line b-b. The Spiritual Force will then tend to get out of Matter, dragging with it atoms of Matter and will start creating a factitious life. This is located in the line A-A, which touches Matter and encompasses it. As it continues its evolution, the Force will produce an etherification close to Matter. The line B-B represents this state. After that, the Astral will be free and will emerge from Matter as depicted by lines C-C and D-D.

Since the Astral is derived from Matter, it is subject to the laws of Matter. Now that it has been etherized, it is subject to the alternatives of the variable attraction and repulsion. It is born and it dies, though its span of life is longer and more durable than that of physical Matter.

Once the Astral is liberated from Matter, it is subject to the divers currents of the physical world. The Initiate who has command over these currents can provoke any atmospheric state of Matter that he desires. For example, he can cause rainfall by evocation. When Jesus' apostles prayed to God to fight a period of dryness and bring about rain, it was not God who acted; it was the power of their prayer that moved the astral currents, mastered them, and produced a condensation in a physical mode.

The Magician makes use of the Quaternary in his evocations. In the circle that he has previously traced as a protection, he draws a cross. In this instance, the cross is the symbol of the Quaternary, for it separates the circle into 4 parts and is thus resolved in the Unity. Magic is the action of physical Man on the astral plane, and whether the cross is drawn in the circle or placed under it ♀, the domination of Unity over the Quaternary, or the latter's

resolving in   Unity, is expressed in
both cases.

The cross of Malta and of the Templars ⊠ does not express the same quaternary. Here, it is neither the physical nor
the astral plane that is depicted, but the mental plane, whose
quaternary is composed of four triangular formations. But we
shall return to this subject further on.

This, brethren, was a general outline of the symbolic meaning
and the practical value of the Astral Quaternary. You have already studied the Unity and the Binary. Here you should not
forget that everything emanates from the Unity and everything
returns to it. Note too that the Law of Unity is not a mere fantasy,
for everything in the Astral Quaternary is so intimately bound
that the existence of Matter is necessary for the existence of Force,
and the existence of Equilibrium is necessary to both the above
Principles.

When we say that the Quaternary will be resolved into the Unity,
be sure that the Great Problems have begun to be formulated and
that the comprehension of this fact will lead us to the perception
of a higher truth: the Divine Trinity, the Trinity in Unity.

Let us meditate and work. It is by this means alone that we shall
acquire knowledge, that 'the scales will fall from our eyes' and
that the Light will become manifest.

Third Speech by D. Semelas

On Magic

(2 / 11 / 1911. Cairo, Egypt)

In my previous talks on the study of the Astral, I spoke to you of the occult Unity, of the Binary, and of the Quaternary. Now that we know this theory, let us try to delve deeper into it and apply it to the study of the Pentagram. This symbol is of very great significance and is very powerful in the astral plane. But before I go into an explanation of it, let us first see the different kinds of adaptation of the Astral – this median region between the Spirit and Matter – that were made in the past and are still made today.

You may ask of what use is the knowledge of the astral to an Initiate. This knowledge has two aims: The first is to enable the Initiate, by meditation, to have a concept of the Invisible, to unite himself with the entities that occupy this plane, to get to know its constitution, and to receive the opinions of Superior Spirits. And all this can be achieved while the Initiate remains in his physical body without release from it (exteriorization). The second aim is to enable the Initiate to release himself from the bonds of his physical body, enter the astral plane, see the beings that live in it, and get to know and understand what takes place there. All this can be achieved without the assistance of his sight or any other of his human physical senses.

Let us momentarily stop at the second aim and let us see how this release and 'trip' of the Spirit to that region can be realized. Astral exteriorization has been known and practised since all time both among ancient and modern peoples. We shall divide it into two distinct categories: 1) exteriorization in an active mode and 2) exteriorization in a passive mode. The first comprises a) the state of being a student (Initiate) and b) the state of being a Master. The second category comprises exteriorization a) with direct reflection and b) with indirect reflection.

We shall now examine these different categories and subdivisions. Exteriorization in a passive mode with indirect reflection is found as a phenomenon among certain persons who manage to get into a kind of ecstasy by absorbing narcotics. When in this state, these persons have visions of incoherent and false images. These have been called 'hallucinations' but this term is not correct. Although incoherence is the particular characteristic of

17

these visions, although the state that these persons are in is not normal, they have still penetrated into a part of the Astral, and what they see is real. I shall describe to you the case of a young girl whose visions were of this category of phenomena. In her sleep at night, she would see beings that surrounded her and threatened her with death. She would then see women beside her who had come to console her and who promised to protect her. In the beginning she was strongly affected by these visions, but she gradually got used to them and was even able to almost take pleasure in this astral nightmare. This state of things eventually wore her out and she fell ill. If the experts of science had examined her, they would have found her hysterical. Hysteria is the term that serves to describe what is beyond the competence of official science. It is a functional not an organic injury. The organs are not attacked, but the regular functioning of the organism is hindered and paralysed. The doctor's inability to cure it is due to the fact that it is impossible for him to give prognosis concerning an illness if no injury exists on the body. The young girl was disturbed because she was in passive ecstasy and so perceived incoherent inferior things, which influenced her to such a point as to become impressed on her brain. In this manner, when she woke up, she could remember what she had seen in her vision of the lower astral plane.

Exteriorization in passive mode with direct reflection is a state in which one has consciousness of all that exists and is part of the astral plane, a state in which one has a vision of it from a distance. This is produced by the result of auto-suggestion or of the influence of a visible 'operator' (magnetist or hypnotist) or of an invisible being that acts on the 'subject' and directs it in the astral plane. As an example, I shall mention the case of a young person who was put to artificial sleep. She saw a young man direct her to a great number of places and make her penetrate into them. When she woke up, she remembered what she had seen during her trip, accompanied by her young fiancé. She could describe the houses that she had visited and portray the persons she had seen playing cards round a table, and she even gave a great number of details that were checked and found to be exact. There is no mistake about it; this young person had indeed seen, and very well at that. Her Spirit had been exteriorized and had been released from its body due to the effect of the influence of the Will of another person. It thus became subject to the domination of this other Will. But because it was passive, it lacked the power to choose which place to go to but blindly carried out the commands given to it.

Let us now pass on to exteriorization in active mode. It is divided in that of an adept and that of a master. This is true realization in this vast domain of the Astral. The exteriorization of the adept to the astral plane is a voluntary one. In the beginning, the Initiate is directed by a visible or invisible guide that makes him get to know this plane, directs him in it and prepares him towards mastery over it. This manner of exteriorization to the astral does not provoke any injury as the above mentioned examples do – those in passive mode – which always have dire results.

But why are the exteriorizations in passive mode always dangerous, whereas the others are not? The former are dangerous because, as in the first example given, the state of ecstasy is the consequence of a non-normal sleep and, as in the second example given, the subject is under the yoke of a Will that is superior to her own. Therefore her receptive and passive state takes everything that is imposed on her and her body receives the repercussion of the violence of the 'operator's' Will. The Spirit no longer has freedom of action and in this way injuries and physical illnesses may ensue.

As regards exteriorizations in active mode, here sleep is natural. The body rests and the Spirit travels to the astral domain, learns about it, sees it and seeks what is of interest to it. It transmits everything to the brain and impresses it so that, upon awakening, the person in question remembers everything they saw and did. No particular diet is needed; both the Adept and the Master can eat anything and lead an ordinary life.

Mastery - the dream of every adept – is the summit of conscious exteriorization. In this state, the Master sees their body lying on the bed. With lightning speed he transports himself to whatever place he desires for the research that he wishes to make. He can act on all his being and return to his body whenever he wishes to. One who has the faculty of mastering the Astral and the forces that act in it is really in possession of enormous power, which is at the full disposal of his Will. However, certain conditions are indispensable in order to attain this result. The Master must have reason as well as well balanced vital faculties, and he must be truly free. No passive person can aspire to such favours, for here exteriorization is the result of one's own will through personal impulse during sleep, which is neither artificial nor imposed by others.

A little more than a hundred years ago there was a lot of fuss over magnetism that had just been discovered. Since then and thanks to a number of experiments, there has been proof of the existence of an etheric substance that has an impact on the body, the soul, and even on the Spirit (in the sense that one spirit can influence another by means of this agent). In order to explain to you what

19

I maintain concerning the theories of the Astral, we shall use the experiments made by our predecessors so as to be certain of the veracity of the results.

When magnetism is used as a healing agent and is guided by spiritual will and a pure desire, it is harmless to Man. It is continuously generated within us by the pressure exerted by the Spiritual Force on Matter through the nervous system. A truly astral fluid incessantly issues from the organs of the human body and every nerve- terminal is a projector of this fluid.

If your hand touches a person at a certain point, you will both feel a sensation that is the result of this physical touch - an astral communication. The best proof of the existence of this agent is that even if you do not see the movement of the person who touches you, you will still be conscious that the movement has been made. This is because, by means of the nervous system, the astral fluid has reached the brain. The brain is in direct communication with all the members of the body through a nerve conductor that transmits sensation to the brain. The whole body is covered by a network of nerves and the extremities of the members are the terminal points of this organism. It is through these that the astral fluid is released. When a person contacts another, he/she transmits to the other what his/her body produces. It is a spiritual-material-etherification; it is the astral fluid.

We can distinguish two kinds of transmission:1) simple, without any continuity of spiritual vibrations, and 2) with continuity of vibrations. In the first case, transmission is made for cures through magnetism. You surely know that when someone feels pain in any part of their body, if hands are laid at the very place where the pain is, the pain eases. This is produced by the impact of astral release, which is at first projected by the person who magnetizes and then is driven into the part that has been afflicted and so re-establishes the astral action and accomplishes the cure. This of course depends on the equilibrium of the 'operator'. In the second case, a person who wishes to make his Will felt by another who is at a more or less great distance away, makes use of this mediator which serves as a vehicle so as to transmit a thought or bring about a cure from a distance.

The astral fluid does not escape from the body only from the extremities of the members or from the projecting organs, such as the eyes, but it radiates over all the surface of the body and is projected outwards at the rate that the spiritual-material action is produced. When the Initiate wishes to communicate and impose his will at a distance, it is through the radiation of the whole of his astral that he can manage to transmit his desire and do what he has decided to do. I will later give you certain indispensable details on this subject and practice.

You now have some information regarding this active agent that we do not see; we only feel its effects. The ancient Initiations knew all about it, and Martinés de Pasqually made use of it.

Let us now see of what usefulness the astral is to Man. Even when fully awake, if the Initiate makes certain preparations and uses certain formulas, he can manage to get into contact with the Astral and the beings that dwell in it. By condensation of this intermediary, he can see the entities, order them, impress them or, on the other hand, be ordered and act according to their Will. When the Initiate acts as described in the first instance, that is, when he is obeyed and when the spirits carry out his orders, this science is called High Magic. In the opposite case, which is but the **magic** of a malevolent ignorance, it is the Black Magic done by the sorcerer who becomes the tool of base astral entities, which command him.

During ceremonies of High Magic, the Magician follows certain preparatory rites in detail and makes use of symbols. These are indispensable so as to attract the spiritual element, which becomes manifest by astral condensation. By exerting his Will, the Magician acts on the spirits and the powers that he has evoked. He is their absolute master; he sees and commands them, and his orders are carried out. Among the symbols that he uses during his evocations, there is none more powerful than the Pentacle or Pentagram, the corresponding knowledge of which explains the mysteries of all the planes and all the initiatic adaptations: Alchemy, Magic, etc. This symbol has the power to fetter any spirit and, when used by a learned 'operator', because it is a sign of divine power in Creation, it brings terror to the astral domain and subjects all the beings found there to the one who holds and has knowledge of it.

In Black Magic, the ceremonies, rites and preparations are totally different from the practices of the Magic of Light. In the latter, the Pentacle is held upright, whereas in Black Magic it is held upside down. The signatures of the genii are reversed as also the names and signs. Everything done is meant to attract the influence of the spirit of disorder, of incoherence, and of evil.

In a pact that has been previously made, the sorcerer is not the master of these evil entities that he evokes; he is their servant; <u>he carries out their Will and they make his desire come true.</u>

Note that there is a great difference between their Will and his desire as regards the eventual action. A lot of persons are sorcerers without meaning to be and they later become sorcerers through

21

habit. They have no knowledge of Occult Philosophy but have seen or possess some wizard's book of so-called spells, with alluring titles and infallible recipes, such as to become loved, to discover treasures, etc. They imagine that in order to acquire magical power, it is enough to pronounce certain bizarre words or utter incomprehensible phrases and thus be able to give orders and be served by spirits. They feel very brave and courageous, draw the circle – or even forget to draw it at all – and inscribe signs that they do not understand. They enter the circle, like powerful warriors, holding the sword in one hand and the wand in the other, and begin their evocations. They may be able to see or they may not, but the mere utterance of certain words and formulas has some result, which in most cases is bad. There are many examples that can be cited. This temerity, to dare carry out operations whose importance one does not know, was, is, and will always be the surest means that leads to certain loss. Absolute ignorance of these matters is the sorcerer's characteristic. After his infernal evocations, he is overcome by vices and commits the monstrosities of the entities that visit him. If he is not subjected to serious illnesses or organic perturbations, he is under the yoke of evil genii and base entities of the Astral. He ends his life in misery, full of horrible nightmares and eventually kills himself.

It is therefore the Initiator's duty to prepare the Initiate so that he may have knowledge of these matters. All those who come to Initiatic Societies seeking for the Truth will find it. They will have the joy of knowing and practising this alluring attraction towards the Invisible. But serious study must precede this, for the Initiator must indicate the road to be followed – and it is a long and hard road.

We shall study these phenomena and the causes that provoke accidents; we shall learn, by purely physical means, about the force that acts. And while on the mystic path, we shall be able, by conscious release during natural sleep, to have a perception of what exists in that region, of its laws and of what can be of use to us.

This result is the outcome of work and of the Initiate's perfection, together of course with the permission of the Invisible.

Fourth Speech by D. Semelas

On the Psychical **Senses**

(10 / 1911. Cairo Egypt)

You surely remember that in my previous speech I mentioned releases (exteriorizations) to the astral plane, their classification, various cases of possession, and mastery over this plane, which is superior to the physical one. It is a plane of etherized Substance and in it Force is freely manifest. There, everything evades our physical senses, though we have direct contact with this plane by means of our invisible or psychical senses. I also spoke to you about Man's communication with the beings that live in the Astral, by means of the practice of Magic.

I shall proceed to explain to you the manner in which you can acquire the necessary power for your evocation, and how you can come in contact with all the beings of the plane in question. But before I do so, let us see what our relations with it can be, how and in what way we feel its influence daily, in what form do we see its inhabitants, and how the reality of this plane is manifest.

The astral plane certainly exists for every person and we can all have perception of it, either awake or asleep. Although its reality cannot be checked by instruments or the physical senses, we can have conscience of it thanks to the psychical sensibility that we are all susceptible to feeling.

When awake, by means of which organs can we have the sensation of the existence of the astral? When we find ourselves among individuals whose evolution is not advanced and as such, is of truly inferior mentality, we feel a certain psychical discomfort. When we meet a person for the first time, we immediately submit to and in turn make that person also submit to an astral influence. Both of us feel a sentiment of sympathy or antipathy in a lesser or greater degree. This sentiment is not the result of physical contact, due to sensations of sight, taste, hearing or touch. It is due to the psychical perception that pro-

23

vides Man with conscience, by setting his psychical senses into action. These last, contrary to the physical senses, can never lead him to error. These invisible senses have the faculty of making Man feel everything that is not related to the physical plane. They are of three different kinds: hearing, sight, and a general psychical sensation. Their seat is located in the breast, and more particularly in the heart.

How do these astral or psychical senses function? During sleep and in a state of dreaming, our senses of sight and hearing are activated. In a state of wakefulness, only the general psychical sensation derived from the heart is active. Consequently, suggestion, telepathy, transmission, attraction and all spontaneous or provoked influences manifested in this state of wakefulness are effectuated by psychical means that result from the astral contact.

What other means do we also have so as to feel the influence of the Astral?

When asleep, Man has dreams that are derived from his impressions of the day, or again sees things that have no relation to these impressions. The origin of both is wholly due to his astral vision. How do we consider these two kinds of phenomena? In the first case, is it a fact that the actions of the day are formations that exist in the astral or just impressions registered in the brain, which present themselves to our memory during sleep? The actions that we do and the thoughts that we emit during the day are not able to impress the brain to such a point, but they do leave a trace on the astral plane. I shall explain to you the theory concerning this phenomenon: You all know where this fluid is derived from – this fluid that fills the void and is the universal mediator. It is derived from the Astral. In Man too, the Spirit acts on Matter and produces this agent. Once it has been produced, on what parts of the human organism does it in turn act? It acts on the nervous system, which is an organ specially created either to manifest this agent or to have command over it. Every action that Man does, every movement, every emission of thought, everything – whatever its plane, physical, moral or intellectual - produces vibrations that affect the nervous system. The vibration 'astralizes' Matter and registers everything that has been done and thought on this mediating plane. In this manner, all around the person who has provoked them, in his/her astral atmosphere, these formations remain for a certain length of time, about a day or more, and are likely to be seen and perceived. Man is thus able during his sleep to see again these astral clichés that he has produced. Consequently it is not the impression given to the brain that makes these clichés reappear, nor is it the Spirit that has kept these memories. However, the Spirit, released from the physical body and wandering in the Astral all around its body, sees and remembers. It reviews what it has done, it sees once again the faces of persons with whom it has spoken when it was attached to its body, remembers conversations and in a word, it sees a detailed picture of what it has lived through, and facts whose physical impress has been registered on the astral plane.

Dreams that have no relation with actions and impressions of the day can be of three different natures. In the first case, when the Spirit, released from its body, travels in the Astral, it may come across vibrations of actions made or events that took place in distant places. In this way, it is impressed. When it wakes up, it may remember having assisted in certain curious events. Sometimes, the spirit meets other spirits; they communicate and exchange thoughts. Upon awakening, the person remembers having seen a certain friend or having heard certain news.

In the second case, the Spirit that has been initiated travels in the Astral, fully conscious of what it sees and hears. It analyses, is capable of judging, and can go wherever it pleases. It voluntarily transmits its impressions to the brain so as to recall them upon awakening.

The third case is the nightmare. It comes as the result of very great nervous excitement or is caused by a state due to the absorption of a great quantity of food or drink. It is not produced by any impression of the Spirit but by the effect of the astral on the nervous system. In this state, Man sees beings trying to strangle him, horrible animals, or again whatever he can imagine as most hideous. This phenomenon is explained as follows: the extreme nervous excitement caused by inebriety or the absorption of too much food produces an effect that corresponds to being physically carried away. It is represented in the astral plane, and Man makes unconscious evocations that provoke a coagulation of the Astral and attract elementals and other impure beings of this plane, which momentarily take possession of his body. These disorders of the nervous system have very dire results. The beings that come to trouble Man's sleep and cause nightmares can be seen by the Magician, whose evocation is a conscious one.

The Magician who makes an evocation is obliged to enclose himself within a protective circle. This is not because he runs any danger from the superior spirits that he evokes, but because he wishes to protect himself from the inferior and incoherent entities that swarm in the astral plane. Ignoble beings can present

25

themselves and try to frighten him so as to make him leave his circle and thus have him at their mercy. The role of the circle is to serve as an astral rampart to the Magician and scare away these elementals.

In order to be able to make an evocation, the Magician should not be in a normal state. He should be driven by some stimulant – coffee, alcohol, tea, ether, hashish, nicotine, etc., that is, by some substance that causes a nervous over-stimulation. You observe that the state required for an evocation is similar to the one that provokes nightmares to the person who has drunk or eaten too much. The Magician voluntarily causes this over-stimulation of the nerves in order to provoke an astral condensation, to see entities, and command them. The state he is in permits him to be fearless and enables him to push back all evil entities.

On the other hand, the one who is drunk or has eaten too much, due to this very nervous over-stimulation, involuntarily condenses the Astral, without making any evocation. He thus allows the elementals to approach him, feels their influence and is in the hold of nightmares from which he is saved only by waking up, that is, when his Spirit returns to his body. If he falls asleep again, the chain is formed once more and the nightmares reappear. He wholly recovers only when, upon awakening, he walks around for a few minutes until the astral coagulation dissolves completely.

It should be quite understood that I take full responsibility for the theories that I present to you. I am authorized to tell you all this through personal experience. These ideas may have already been expressed by those who have dealt with the subject. I leave it to your good sense to draw the suitable conclusions in accordance with the spirit of our Order.

We should not deny the existence of the Astral. We all feel its impact, and the present speeches can permit you to study in what way we can establish well- balanced relations between the physical and the astral planes. We shall thus know what we must do so as to avoid the unfavourable action of evil entities and attract the good and superior spirits from whose influence we can only profit. They will enlighten us concerning this domain and help us acquire superior initiatic instruction.

The Initiate tries to communicate with the astral plane because of the importance of the knowledge that he can derive from it. He does not desire any material profit but an intellectual one, whose result is far from insignificant to anyone who knows. It is indeed very agreeable to follow a path that leads to the mastery of this plane. This mastery provides its chosen one with the mysterious key that will open the door of secrets to him. He will then learn the most marvellous and noble things, whose reality he cannot even suspect while still in the physical plane. He will then possess power that flatters him, and from then on will be able to act for the common good and be of assistance to his brethren, physically, morally and spiritually.

Now that we have proved the existence of the Astral, let us examine its usefulness to the Initiate.

1) The Initiate who has the qualities required in order to have contact with the inhabitants of the astral plane, the Initiate who has an intense desire and a pure heart, must do everything possible so as to acquire knowledge of this superior plane that governs intellectual, moral, psychical and physical forces. He must then try to apply his knowledge in the present plane for his own benefit and for that of all others.

2) Once the Initiate is master of the astral plane, he has greater facility in speeding up his own evolution.

3) He can perform acts (works) that will render both him and others happy. At first these will be intellectual, but later, through practice and adaptation, they will be morally, physically, and socially beneficial. He will understand laws that were unknown to him. This new knowledge will reveal to him a number of mysteries. When he crosses the threshold, he will become a new being who possesses the knowledge of the great mysteries of Nature and the allegories of the Cabbalah. He will have the solution to all the problems set in his Spirit and possess that most precious good – moral consolation, evenness of temper in his affections, and peace of heart. Moreover, in his 'trips', the Initiate will see unknown places that will attract him by the beauties found there. He will go wherever he desires and rapidly get knowledge that would have required years to acquire in a mere physical body. He can learn the mysteries of Man's life and get to know Man perfectly well. Then, through his own willpower, he can impose, suggest, and emit ideas that will become a reality for the good of others. His life will truly be a life with a mission which, together with intellectual satisfaction, will provide him with a priceless spiritual harvest.

Now that the Initiate has been informed of all these advantages, he must also remember that the person who wishes to enter this domain and acquire mastery over it, must possess certain qualities. He must have a resolute will, invincible strength, and indomitable courage, for when he tries to cross the threshold of this plane, a gigantic green dragon – the guardian – will stand before him and try to prevent him from entering. At that moment he must make use of his courage, which has not so far been put to the test. He must vanquish the dragon and cross the threshold. After that, courage is useless to him; he will not need it any more. The greatest step has been taken; from now on he will need only perseverance. He must be impassive and not allow himself to get distracted. He will thus have complete control over his intellect. If he does not want the chain to break, he must keep his heart pure, have only good intentions and make deliberate use of his power only for a good cause. If he abused this power, he would end up, like in the allegory, wasting all the strength acquired at such pains and would irrevocably lose it.

In conclusion, let us add that whoever wishes to reign in this domain must be able to express an opinion on everything that he sees and hears, solve the questions that usually cause frustration, adapt his knowledge to what he wishes to carry out, and set everything that he comprehends about occult secrets for the benefit of humanity.

On Good and **Evil**

(10 /1911. Cairo, Egypt)

In my previous speech we examined the principal ways of acquiring the practice of exteriorization in astral body. On this subject I told you that the person who wished to try these practices should be prepared from all points of view: spiritual, moral and psychical.

Today, I take the opportunity to speak to you about the psychical qualities and defects which - under the general denomination of Astral Morality – are classified as Good and Evil.

I shall not deal with the subject in a spiritual sense; I do not want to classify Spirits as good or evil, since in their essence they are not so. Good and Evil are found only in the astral of every Spirit. We shall try to find out what is Good and what is Evil, and then whether these qualities and defects exist in astral Essence.

A number of great Theosophists have written treatises under various titles in order to explain Good and Evil. Most of them have presented them from the spiritual point of view. Others have tackled the subject on an inferior level. After a number of compilations and studies on Man, they still did not find the true cause of the existence of Good and Evil and have ended up denying their existence. This is an error. Good and Evil do exist, but they must not be considered as two opposites. They are neither in the physical nor in the spiritual plane. The truth concerning this subject lies only in the median plane, the astral plane.

I shall try to tell you what Good is and prove to you its existence. After study and meditation, you have all observed the Great Harmony that reigns in Nature. I have already drawn your attention to this subject. Today, I once again exhort you to see and discover the Law of Harmony that governs everything. You all know that the stars are beings that follow their course in the Universe with perfect mathematical precision. You know that the Sun, which gives us light, and the Earth, on which we live, follow this same Law of the Great Universal All. We can also see that the atoms that compose our own body, as well as that of every living being, follow the same Law, and that everything in the Universe, just as in Man, functions and works towards a determined end. After seeing harmony in movement, we see it in

29

colour, and after studied concentration we see it in the vibrations emitted in the Universe, and we shall then understand the Universal musical Harmony.

But what is the role of harmony and what does it tend to? Its role is to bring the plurality of beings back to perfect Unity. This is indeed a Sublime Work. The thought of it alone leads to concentration and to the adoration of God through His works.

What is the Law of Creation? It is the Law of Harmony, and everything, absolutely everything in the Universe is subject to this Law. Every action made that conforms to this Law is classified as Good. Every action committed outside this Law, every discordant sound, every dissonance or broken tone, everything outside Harmony is Evil. Evil cannot exist, move or live, for the Law of Harmony will bring it back to the path of life and may eventually annihilate it altogether so as to remake it harmonious. It will then be part of the Good.

An example: Take the soldiers at their training camp. They must all make movements in complete harmony, following a determined manner and time. In the beginning they move their weapons right and left, and the movements are as many as the number of soldiers. The sergeant follows them and punishes them accordingly. The soldiers pay greater attention and try to carry out the movements in complete harmony. Here you have an example of Good and Evil.

Any movement of disharmony is Evil. When the harmonious vibrations arrive from the Astral, they bring about the punishment of such actions in the soul of Man, as well as in the Universe. When the acts of Man are made to conform to harmony, then the victory of Good is re-established in the Astral. So you see that Evil is indeed done, but it exists only momentarily, for in the end it is absorbed. Good is always victorious.

Let us now see a more concise theory of the idea of Good and Evil. Every accomplished act, every emitted vibration in the physical or astral planes, every movement that does not conform to Universal Harmony – which is the Unique Law of the Works of the Creator – is Evil. Consequently, every movement, vibration or act committed in the physical or astral planes that conforms to the Unique Law of Harmony is Good.

What does the theory of Good and Evil in the Astral prove to us and what is its usefulness? This theory proves the existence of spiritualized dynamic agents that are charged with the maintenance of the Unique Law of Harmony. These agents check and bring back to order the discordant tones, the dissonances in Universal Harmony, and hinder the disharmony of vibrations and all revolt against the Unique Universal Law. Agents of Evil also exist and the Saviour mentioned them when He spoke of demons well exerted in Evil and of angels at the service of Good. What we have seen bears witness in favour of this theory. Besides we become aware of the reality of these agents through their physical and astral effects.

One who aspires and is called to work in the astral plane must be well balanced. In order to achieve this balance, one needs to know only one of these powers so as to communicate with the beings of this plane. But one needs also know the origin of both agents so as to be able to have command over them and master them. In other words, one must know both Good and Evil. The full knowledge of these two agents will lead to the realization of Harmony and Unity. The Magician – absolute master of the astral plane – will be able to acquire brilliant lights and incalculable benefits.

I do not preach to you the appeal of Good and the horror of Evil. Instead I draw you attention to the practical usefulness that the zealous Initiate can obtain from the science of Good and Evil.

When we start practising, we shall examine the nature of these agents; we shall learn how to attract some and repel others. Then the Initiate can call himself an authority on Good and Evil.

On the Astral and **Talismans**

(29 /11 / 1911. Cairo, Egypt)

I recently spoke to you about exteriorizations in astral body and divided them into 3 categories: the passive, the active auto-exteriorization, and the active one. The first is that of mediums and spiritualists of today; the second is that of the Initiate-disciple in the science of the astral plane, and the third is that of mastery over this plane.

I have already explained to you these various states and means. I shall not refer again to the first state, for it is a false one. The subject that has been put artificially to sleep is in an absolutely passive state. We know the means used and also know that those who are subjected to them attract the direst effects for their immediate future.

Let us pass on to the other categories. The active auto-exteriorization is the stage of learning the science of the astral plane. It is the principle of the conquest of this plane. But there are certain means necessary to make us acquire this ability. We shall examine these first, and then try to have a true concept of the theory and practice of mastery over the Astral.

To begin with, brethren, what is a Talisman? It is any object on which a strong will has been imposed and fixed through certain means and rites that we shall describe. Today, the talisman is an object of commerce. It is traded for quite a substantial sum, according to its so-called power. This is pure exploitation, considering that the occult value of such a talisman is absolutely nil.

A talisman is not some metal plaque or a piece of parchment on which circles, pentacles, signs and seals, etc. are etched. No, it is not. A talisman of real value and real power must be made by a Master in accordance with some rites and by following certain formulas that have been revealed and proved correct by practice.

There are three kinds of talismans, for here again we come across the Law of the Ternary. This is the principal Law, which is divided into three integral parts.

1) If the Initiate wants to make a person feel some sensation whatever, he takes an object, a piece of parchment or a metal plaque, and imposes his Will on it according to what he wishes to be felt and focuses (fixes) this Will by means of certain signs. When the person for whom

this talisman is destined comes into contact with it, he/she is subject to the Will of the 'operator' and feels everything that the latter wanted to impose on him/her. This fact corresponds to the experiments of Magnetism and Hypnotism.

2) The talisman pertaining to the second category is one that has such virtue (power) as to allow the persons wearing it to exteriorize in a state of wakefulness. In a way they spring from their physical body and, in a kind of ecstasy, are able to see and know distant horizons.

In the well-known Arab stories of marvels, which even today can be found in the corner bookstore and which amuse people with their fantastic complications, there is the story of Khalima. It tells of a man who found a talisman and placed it on his forehead. Immediately there appeared before him the vision of a mountain in whose depths lay hidden treasures. This man, who was the King's son, saw all this, as well as many other marvellous things that he could not have seen physically, and started travelling so as to discover this fantastic mountain. His talisman acted as his guide and he eventually arrived at the place indicated. He found an opening to the cave, entered it, saw the treasure and took it away with him.

I do not mean by this that the role of such a talisman is to help discover hidden treasures. By making use of such talismans, one can see a lot of other things besides.

3) The talisman pertaining to the third category is that which belongs to the Initiate who has had the patience to go through the stage of learning. He then possesses it and wears it, and thanks to the power that has been fixed upon it, he can exteriorize during his ordinary sleep. He can wander about in the Astral and have full conscience of everything that takes place at a particular area that he desires to visit. Finally, the Initiate acquires power in this plane – in a word, he has mastery over it. The astral auto-extriorization at the stage of learning is not effectuated by the disciple's own Will but by the Will that he borrows from his Initiator. This Will is impressed on an object. But once the Initiate attains mastery, the object no longer has any power other than his own. In the beginning, with the help of the talisman, the Initiate releases his astral body, together with his spiritual Essence. He is fully conscious of everything he does; he travels and acts.

After spending some time in exercise, the Initiate travels in the Astral with his Initiator. The talisman is the goal of his Initiation. When he is given it, he wears it all the time and by studying the effect that ensues, he can tell whether his Initiator is truly a Master of not. The Initiate feels a Will within him, it is that of his Initiator. He strengthens this Will by means of his exercises; he can perceive the astral plane better as well as his own physical body lying at rest. This is a great step forward and his quest is answered by allegories of revelation. It is this passage from the physical

33

plane to the astral one, which I shall later explain to you.

Gradually the talisman loses its power in a degree commensurate to the Initiate's gain of power. By the time the power of the talisman is spent, the Initiate has become Master and can even have his own adepts.

The Initiate can now start travelling in the astral without being escorted by his Master. Since he possesses his talisman, he no longer needs his Master. He eventually acquires mastery without having to submit to passiveness, such as is imposed to the pupils by 'operators'. From then on the talisman is but a memento of his Initiator. Now that the Initiate has become a Master, he can begin his real work in the astral and sidereal plane. But he must not feel any pride in his success, for pride brings disharmony, a discordant and dissonant note that can make him lose forever the power that he acquired with such difficulty.

On the Astral **(contd)**

(6 /12 /1911. Cairo, Egypt)

In my previous speeches I mentioned to you the possibility of astral 'trips'. I pointed out the different ways by means of which the Initiate's Spirit is released and can thus have the vision of distant horizons, while all the time his physical body is asleep and lies inert on the bed.

Today I would like to speak to you again about this same possibility, but not from an occult or mystical point of view but from a scientific one.

I have already proved to you the existence of evil in the Astral and, through various instances of experiments, the reality of the phenomena that result from it.

In this our present brief study we shall see how science could prove that the Spirit can become released and leave its physical envelope and how and by what organs this Spirit can continue distributing life to the body while it is in this state.

According to the occultists of antiquity, the exteriorized Spirit remained attached to the human body by a very fine thread of astral fluid issuing from the navel. This theory is not correct, for in ancient times people were ignorant of quite a number of things that have been discovered since, and therefore the medical or other scientific opinions of that time were erroneous. The fact is that the Spirit cannot be attached to the body by the navel. It stands to reason that it can only be attached to the head, which is the seat of the brain and where – as was demonstrated – all the human faculties are located. Besides, all the physiologists and neurologists have admitted that all actions have the brain as their source.

The head is pre-eminently the region where the Spirit dominates. The Spirit transmits its Will and its orders to the organs by means of the brain. Let us have an anatomical view of this organ (the brain) and let us examine how the Spirit can approach or withdraw from it.

!!! lobes of the brain / Pineal gland ? Cerebellum.

You see here a sketch of the brain and its annexes. It is divided into lobes, and the small appendage towards the front is the Pineal Gland. Lower down, you can see the Cerebellum. It is

35

absolutely necessary for you to have an accurate concept of what I present to you, for you must not accept any idea unless you have first analysed and understood it completely.

Now let us see how the Spirit transmits its orders to the body by means of the brain. The Spirit has continuous domination over the two lobes. The cerebellum, independent of the brain, is separated from it during our sleep, whereas it adapts itself in a different manner when we are awake, and is in contact with the brain.

Every will, power, or order that is emitted by the Spirit produces a stimulation in the particular part of the brain which is the seat of the faculty that the Spirit desires to set into action. This part is attached by a thread to the cerebellum, which is a mass of nerve fibres. Thus, the stimulation produced in that particular part of the brain transmits the order to the cerebellum, which in turn transmits it to the nerves. Finally, these last execute the order by setting the corresponding organ in motion.

Two nerves start from the cerebellum. One passes inside the spine and is the spinal cord, whose function is to nourish the muscles. The second is found along the spinal column; it is the Great Sympathetic nervous system, (automatic) whose role is to stimulate movement.

Nourishment of the muscles is carried out as follows: a nervous network sends force to the muscle in question and another nervous network removes the toxic substances that have been formed.

Two nerves are also needed to set an organ in motion; one gives movement whereas the other removes the force towards the brain. The spinal cord nourishes the muscle with force; the sympathetic nerve makes the organ move and the Spirit transmits its Will at times to the one an at times to the other.

There exists a third nervous plexus. This proves the possibility of exit to the Astral; it is the Pneumo-Gastric nerve (automatic). It starts from the centre of the brain and descends down to the lower abdomen. It gives nourishment as well as movement to the heart, lungs, liver, kidneys, intestines, etc.

The domination of the Spirit over the brain is revealed by two active productions – the voluntary and the involuntary action. The voluntary action takes place when the Spirit stimulates a certain part of the brain where a faculty that can become manifest resides. The involuntary action takes place when the stimulus is on a part that has a perpetual impulsive function, such as the production of heartbeats, bowel movement, contraction and dilatation of organs – in a word, whatever pertains to the maintenance of the internal organs of the body.

This is the reason why the pneumo-gastric nerve is directly attached to the brain. If it were attached to the cerebellum – which is separated from the brain during sleep – no internal function could have been possible.

What is the theory concerning sleep? There are many theories, but we shall look at the principal ones. When the cerebellum gets detached from the brain, thus cutting off all communication between it and the nervous system, Man is asleep. The body is at rest, but the heart, just like all other internal organs, keep working. They go on with their functions because they are perpetually directly dependent on the Spirit through the mediation
of the pneumo-gastric nerve whose starting point is the centre of the brain.

Can the Spirit withdraw at a distance from the brain? The Spirit can withdraw from the brain but always remains bound to it at a point – the Pineal gland. By the mediation of this gland it continues to stimulate the brain, which – by means of the pneumo-gastric nerve – will direct the functioning of the internal organs.

The muscles, which depend on the great sympathetic nerve as well as on the spinal cord, do not receive the nourishment of force during sleep. In the state of wakefulness, this nourishment is provided in the degree that it is spent. It is when the muscle works that it is nourished for, if the fluidic force did not arrive immediately and were not commensurate to the muscular effort exerted, any continuous work would be impossible.

For example, if you take hold of a spring at both ends and start pressing them together, you will see that after a few minutes' exercise you hands will be paralysed and you will be unable to continue. If you stop for a few minutes and then resume, you note that you can go on with the exercise. Where has the force come from that allows you to resume? It comes from the nerves that have sent it to your arms when the latter were obliged to stop. This has been scientifically verified.

It is possible for the Spirit to leave the body while the latter is in a state of sleep, for then the Spirit does not have to stimulate so many parts of the brain as it does when the person is awake. All the Spirit's work lies in maintaining he movement of the internal organs. Besides, when asleep, the body does not feel anything and therefore it does not send any impressions to the brain. When a person is awake, it is impossible for the Spirit to withdraw from the body. The brain is continually stimulated, either by the Spirit itself or by external impressions. Moreover, the Spirit has to sustain the body and watch over it.

Why do we shut our eyes when we sleep? Man shuts his eyes because the greatest stimulus between the external world and the brain must cease when the Spirit is released. I repeat, the Spirit should then have to stimulate only a part of the brain – that which maintains the life of the human being. The heart cannot stop beating or the bowels stop working in a certain manner so as to digest the nourishment. Thus the Spirit is free to do what it likes, free to work and to travel in the astral plane.

How can the Spirit transmit what it sees and hears during its distant exteriorization in the astral plane? When we have our eyes open we have knowledge of the form, the size and the quality of things. If we close our eyes, this consciousness ceases and we understand that the nervous stimulation provided by sight is reflected in the astral part of the brain so that the Spirit can read it there. The Spirit does not see the part in question but sees the reflection that is registered in the cerebral mirror.

The brain is the most useful organ. Even if Man were able to live without it, he would act without purpose, would be idiotic and have no notion of what is all around him.

When the Spirit travels in the Astral, it perceives the spiritual aspect of everything presented to it. It transmits this perception through the fluidic thread to the brain, which retains the impression for a certain time. When the person wakes up, this impression becomes manifest as a memory. Then Man remembers having seen and heard, having travelled to certain places, and can make profitable use of the knowledge acquired.

All Initiates agree on the subject of conscious exteriorization of the Spirit in the Astral. Those who had the faculty to do so were neither insane nor ill. Scientifically they were right and what they had seen was normal.

These demonstrations do not only prove the possibility of astral travel, they also set us on the road towards the knowledge of the means to achieve it.

On the Astral **(contd)**

(27 /12 /1911. Cairo, Egypt)

In my previous speech I explained to you the possibility of an exteriorization in astral body. This I did by means of positive science. To this end, I gave you a general outline of the nervous anatomy and mentioned the role of the brain, of the Pineal gland, of the Cerebellum, etc.

I shall add a few words to remind you of it all. In the human organism, the nervous system is divided into two principal nerves. The first is of the same substance as that of the brain. It starts from the cerebellum and follows internally the spinal column. It is the spinal cord, whose role is to nourish the muscles with force (strength). The second is the great sympathetic nerve, which descends in a course parallel to that of the spine, and its function is to make the muscles move.

The internal organs are also nourished and moved by a third nerve, which starts from the centre of the brain. It is called the pneumo-gastric (automatic) nerve. It makes the heart, lungs, bowels, etc. function.

Now that this has been established, let us ask the question: How is sleep obtained? I shall first present to you the scientific theory and then follow it up with mine.

The brain is composed of nervous cells about the form sketched here. Small fibres issue all around these cells. These cells are all superimposed on one another and hold and touch one another. The scientific medical theory is the following: when the cerebral cells relax and are at a distance from one another, sleep ensues. From then on, since the union and contact no longer exist between the cells, the nervous circuit is cut off, the faculties momentarily stop working and the body can rest.

This theory has not been able to be proved as absolutely correct, for experimentation is impossible. This hypothesis was formulated after a superficial examination of the possibility of setting the cells at a distance from one another.

We could accept this theory, but I shall prove to you that the cells separate from one another for other reasons. If the cells did not cut off all contact with one another, concentration on a single subject would be impossible.

When I am dealing with a subject, the particular faculty from which my subject is derived is located in the brain and the corresponding cells will all be in close contact with one another. However, in all the other parts of the brain, where other faculties, alien to the subject, reside, the cells will separate from one another.

You must have seen in the shop-windows of opticians those plaster heads whose skull is divided into small compartments in which the various human faculties are inscribed: one for memory, another for courage, etc. The study of all this forms the science of phrenology. This science was established as a result of a host of observations and verifications. For example, a man was hurt at the forehead and it was observed that he lost the faculty of speech. It was also observed that others who were hit at the very same place on the forehead, all lost the faculty of speech. It was

therefore accepted that the place where the wounds had been inflicted was the seat of the faculty of speech.

Thus, when a person concentrates on a particular subject, all the cells of the other parts of the brain, where the faculty in question does not reside, separate from one another so as to allow the Spirit to act with lucidity and greater ease.

Now I shall present my own theory, which again cannot be proved by experimentation. But I shall also present you with its plausibility.

According to anatomists, the cerebellum is separated from the brain. It is a mass of threads and fibres that end up in nerves. This organ is adapted on the posterior part of the brain. Through it, the Will of the brain is transmitted to the great sympathetic nerve and the result is movement or again, it is transmitted by means through the spinal cord to the vital fluid, which is ceaselessly made to circulate by the Spirit.

During sleep, the cerebellum is separated from the brain and has no contact with it. Proof of this is that a void between these two organs has been observed in persons during sleep. Scientists have observed and verified this but have been unable to explain the reason for it. During sleep then, communication between the brain and the nervous system is cut off. But the person who is asleep may make certain unconscious movements. This is due to a small residue of the nervous fluid contained in the body. It is a kind of deposit that remains in all the nervous plexuses. These movements are not guided by the Will. For example, when the body gets tired in a certain position, it moves round to another one. Still, how are these involuntary movements during sleep explained, since the cells of the brain are separated? This question proves the falsity of the medical theory. The brain never stops working; it is always active. Sleep is caused only due to the lack of contact between the brain and the cerebellum.

Let us now look at another aspect of this question. The reflection of sensation, vision or other effect on the brain is produced by a nervous stimulus. The ocular nerve will be stimulated by every image that crosses the eye. I see you; the ocular nerve is stimulated and transmits this stimulus to the brain. I also have conscience of what I see. I then close my eyes. There is no longer any stimulus and therefore no transmission. Or again, I have a certain brainwave; there is a stimulus; the cerebral nerves work and cannot possibly relax.

If a person is extremely tired, the Spirit leaves the brain and the person becomes comatose, like someone dead. And yet, the heart keeps beating, the lungs, as well as all the other internal organs, go on working, even though the cerebellum has been separated from the brain and all communication between them has been cut off. Why is this so? The internal organs go on working because the pneumo-gastric (automatic) nerve that makes them function is directly dependent on the brain. It starts from the pineal gland and has no connection whatever with the cerebellum. It receives the fluid directly from the brain.

Again, how can this be? Since the brain is inactive and does not process the fluid? The Spirit does not feel fatigue. It knows no time or place. Its work is perpetual and its seat is the brain. Even when it is at a distance from the brain, it is still linked to it by an invisible astral thread. The possibility of this fact can only be proved by radio- telepathy.

At what point is the Spirit linked to the brain? Science gauges this somewhat. It is a particular point from which all functions depart. Science has been obliged to kill quite a number of living beings in order to solve this problem. In their experiments, scientists always observed an alienation preceding death or again, a sudden death. Therefore there was no conclusive evidence.

41

I shall try to make myself clearer. When the cerebellum is separated from the brain, the latter goes on functioning and acts through the pneumo-gastric nerve in order to continue the vital internal nourishment of the body, which it has abandoned while dealing with some external matter, such as spiritual research, etc. The Spirit is released and leaves the brain at rest, while all the time it is still linked to it (if I can use this expression) at this particular point. This point is a conceptive organ of the brain and – as I have already told you – by means of this organ the brain receives the impressions so that when the person wakes up, he/she will have conscience of what the Spirit saw and did during sleep. During its astral travel, the Spirit transmits its impressions to their corresponding centres (locations), such as the auditory, ocular, etc. and upon awakening, the person has an idea of what they heard, saw, etc. in their astral trip.

Science cannot claim that we deviate from the truth since we can prove that our assertions are possible. If this Force is not material, it can very well be at a distance from its physical envelope, see, hear, and then return to it. I do not want to speak to you about dreams according to the scientific point of view, for we are formally opposed to this theory. Since the principle in question is erroneously defined, the result of the research is inevitably equally false.

What we need to know here is:

To feel and know the principal point of the brain where the seat of the Spirit is found or, better still, the point on which the Spirit acts directly.

To know the means by which we can exercise the subtle parts of the brain and render them sensitive to the reflections sent by the Spirit regarding what it saw during its exteriorizations.

To learn what work is needed to be done in the brain so as to manage to travel in the Astral.

Note well that I do not seek to impose any dogmas on you. I do not wish to suggest any ideas to you. I only tell you what I know and my aim is simply to show you a method of developing your faculties, as also to make you understand the possibility of astral travel.

Observe the sketch. It rep-

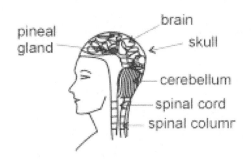

pineal gland

brain

skull

cerebellum

spinal cord

spinal columr

resents approximately a view of the brain as seen from below. You note that almost in the centre there is a kind of cyst. It is the pineal gland. It is this essential point that is of interest to us. This gland is filled with a liquid that looks like water but rapidly evaporates.

It was observed that when an animal was killed during its sleep, this gland was full of the liquid in question whereas if it was killed while awake, the gland was partially full. This liquid is a deposit of the nervous liquid that is meant to maintain the body in life during the absence of the Spirit.

Of what use is this knowledge to the Initiate? The Initiate is interested in this study

1) so as to develop the size of this gland and 2) so as to render these brain centres (localizations) of the intellectual faculties more sensitive to the impressions of astral sight, hearing and touch. In this manner the Initiate will be able to remember the places that the Spirit visited in its astral travels.

How can these results be obtained from a philosophic point of view? If we wish to obtain a result in this direction, it is important to do some exercises that will help develop the pineal gland. One such exercise is to regulate our sleep, that is, go to sleep and wake up at regular hours. Another exercise is the practice of meditation.

How is it that such apparently simple exercises are able to develop such significant faculties? When we focus and fix our thoughts on a subject or on an organ, we have reflex ideas of this thought or organ. If I keep thinking that I have heart trouble, in a short time I shall observe that my thought has acted in a certain manner, that an action or a reflex has been produced, and that I really have got heart trouble.

Meditate. Concentrate you Will on withdrawal to the Astral. This will provoke a certain nervous stimulus that will bring on a congestion or rush of blood on that part of the brain where this faculty resides. The blood is driven to that part and makes it develop and grow. Meditation allows the development of the pineal gland and prepares one for the state of learning (of being a Disciple).

Other secondary exercises will provide you with the means to remember what you see and hear in the Astral.

I do not advise you to draw a black point on the wall and keep staring at it for hours on end. No, because this would only suggest to you all kinds of absurdities and you will end with nothing but sore eyes. This is a wholly passive way of meditating and has nothing to do with Initiation. Instead, try reading something at a great distance or focus all your forces on something far away. In this manner you will develop those parts of the brain that pertain to sight and will manage to have the visual impression of what is distant. This is what the astral trip is all about. For a period of about 5-10 minutes, while in a very normal state, try to distinguish something that is at a great distance. You will acquire a stronger and more sensitive sight.

Again, try to catch conversations carried out some distance away. This exercise – which corresponds to the one of sight - will develop your hearing. You will thus learn to focus a certain faculty at a particular point and examine it thoroughly.

In the Astral, you mainly see and hear; the sense of touch is of no use to you. Its development belongs to the domain of exteriorisation in astral body and later in coagulation.

We now enter into the second branch of the study of the Astral. It is the study of Magic, which is the action and domination of the Spirit over everything external, by the intermediary of the astral fluid.

In conclusion, I advise you to practise developing your faculties so that you may be able to perceive what at present is impossible for you to know. You will thus start practising this priceless Initiation.

I make a point of stressing to you that this is not in the least a matter of auto- suggestion, for you could easily confuse what has just been said with the passive methods of auto-suggestion. All the work must be carried out by the 3 Virtues of the Spirit. This is why knowledge of the topography of your brain is necessary so that you may develop certain of its organs in full consciousness.

Frerers d Orient(Brothers from the East)
Inner Order of the Knights Templars

The Order of Knights Templars

The our lineage of Gnostic Christianity is composed of various "orders," which are something like Tantra Yogas one might find in Vajrayana (Esoteric Buddhism) – hence, the orders are composed of a view, along with teachings and practices that form a vehicle through which something of the enlightenment experience or gnostic experience might transpire. The Order of Knights Templars and Order of St. Mary Magdalene are among the principle orders in our lineage. The Order of St. Mary Magdalene, as its name implies represents a path of devotion to the Divine and Sacred Feminine, the Magdalene Path, and the Order of Knights Templars represents the guardianship of this our Gnostic tradition; and specifically represents an order of the "Knights and Dames of the Holy Grail."

Originally, these two orders represented teachings and practices through which men and women might honor the Holy Bride, the Order of Knights Templars being primarily for men and the Order of St. Mary Magdalene being primarily for women; however, in modern times these orders are open fully to both men and women – though, no doubt, men will have a special understanding of Christ in their experience as men, just as women will have a special understanding of St. Mary Magdalene in their experience as women.

In some legends of the Holy Bride she is said to have a daughter (Sarah) and in others she is said to have a son (Michael), and in some she is said to have "twins," a daughter and a son.

To understand the generation of the Order of Knights Templars the Order of St. Mary Magdalene must be mention, for quite literally it was an order created to guard the Magdalene line of Gnostic Apostolic Succession and is said to be an "old Gnostic Templar lineage." It is a Chivalric Gnostic order that stands independently from other chivalric orders, and by nature is an esoteric chivalric order, for as much as teaching the principles of chivalry and the righteous warrior outwardly, inwardly it teaches the "art of a spiritual warrior," an art of divine theurgy ("the way of the exorcist"), which is used as a means of invisible and spiritual protection of the Gnostic lineage and its initiates, and is extended to people in need of assistance.

Initiation into the Order of Knights Templar is based upon the ceremony of a dubbing of a chevalier (a knight or dame) and the speaking of the Holy Vow of the Order; the key symbols of the Order are the Sword (or Lance) and the Grail, which are used in a Gnostic Mass that reflects a key mystery celebrated in the Order: Hieros Gamos.

The ceremonial robe of the Order is a white robe with a red Templar cross on it and a red cord is worn, and typically black clothing is worn beneath the robe.

Although the Order of Knight Templars is an esoteric and initiatory order, the spiritual wisdom of many of the teachings and practices can be beneficial to the initiate and non-initiate alike.

Blessings
Deon

Union with the Black Madonna and Child

The Black Madonna, Kali Imma, is the Holy Mother of Templars, and the Black Sun, Kali Shemesh, is the face of the Messiah that Templars adore – the face of the Messiah in the Judgment, or face of the Messiah in the Apocalypse.

She is Our Lady of Strength and Judgment, and she is Our Lady of Victory in Battle, and she is Our Lady of Healing and Granting Boons; she is the Divine Lady of the people, not the popes – she exalts the humble and brings low the proud, she bestows blessings on those who love her, but is a bane to those who despise her. She is black to those who are distant from her and do not know her as yet, but she is white brilliance to her lovers who are near to her, pure sweetness and light !

In this are given keys for the Templar initiates to contemplate in order to gain knowledge and understanding, and grow in wisdom – and we shall say, "She is Mother Wisdom, Mother Sophia." Therefore, if you wish to know her read and contemplate the Books of Wisdom, such as Proverbs and The Perfect Thunder Mind, and pray to her for instruction and understanding; when she chooses, she will reveal herself to you.

Of her Holy Son, you must know that he is White Brilliance in the center of the Black Earth, and he is the Dark Radiance beyond the Kingdom of Heaven – if you seek to know and understand him, then rise up, honor your holy vow, and defend the City of God and Holy Grail, and if you fall in battle know that you will be counted among the Blessed Dead in the Body of Sophia Stellarum, for Divine Grace will uplift you and you shall attain victory to be called
"Israel."
***

There is a secret to be spoken: Abraham was the first Templar and Sarah the first Crone Mother, the daughter of Kali Imma – by Melchizedek, King of Salem, he was dubbed and she was honored. Amen and amen – truth is spoken!

***

A lad once sought to become a Templar and inquired of an old man where he might find the Knights Templars; the sage replied, "Go south, and follow along the Path of the Dragon; there is a holy palace in the south in which their Holy Queen dwells, and there you will find some from among their Holy Order standing guard and in worship."

Another holy sage once said, "The Queen of Sheba lives in the South."
***

This is all that we may say openly regarding Our Lady and her Holy Child – if you wish to know more then you must be dubbed and honor your holy vow, and when you return victorious from battle, as a tried spiritual warrior, then perhaps you might inquire of a Priest-King or Priestess- Queen, or perhaps of a Sacred Tau, and if the Holy Spirit is willing they will tell you secret mysteries mouth-to-ear, assuming you know them already.

Union with the Black Madonna and Child Practice

If you wish to take up Union with the Black Madonna, then you must seek her blessing, for only she gives the empowerment through which union with her is attained. On the New Moon go out and gaze upon the night sky and the stars, and as you pray and meditate, let your gaze be directed southward, allowing your soul and spirit to follow the Milky Way, the Path of the Dragon; if the Gate Keeper allows you passage and the Spirit of Yahweh grants you a vision, then it is given to you to take up Union with Kali Imma – if not, then you must wait and go out again on the next New Moon seeking your vision from the Spirit of the Dragon, the Spirit of Yahweh.

Alternatively, set your attention upon your brow, focusing in the center of your head, the center of your brain, and intone the Blessed Name of Yeshua[1] Messiah into this center until your sight opens into the World of the Holy Spirit – when it opens you are called to take up Union with the Black Madonna.

If you wish to gain insight into Kali Imma, meditate upon Ain, no-thingness, and this will bring you into her acquaintanceship – in this way, too, you might be called by her to seek union with her, all as she wishes!

This is the holy vow and view of those who seek Union with Kali Imma: "All as She wishes."

These are practices in preparation for Union with Kali Imma.

Meditation Image: She is Radiant Darkness clothed in Golden Light, with jewels of the Five Essential Lights in her light vestures, and she is enthrones upon a Great Black Dragon, with Four Great Serafim in the form of Jeweled Dragons surrounding her, with St. Michael standing guard and leading worship as Maggid Cohen Ha-Gadol, and with countless holy ones and angels of El Elyon in attendance.

Here Holy Son is enthroned upon her lap, also having a Divine Body of Dark Radiance, and wearing the same light vestures; she and he wear diamond crowns, radiant with the White Brilliance of Supernal Glory.

Surrounding her Light Palace are countless abodes of Light and Darkness, and beyond her abode is that Great Void into which only her Holy Son and his Holy Bride can gaze – be humbled therefore, and do not seek to gaze into that Dwelling Place, lest perchance you be stricken with madness, such as was the Adversary who sought to make himself the Most High.

The Union

Envision your Body of Light as formed of most subtle translucent light, completely hollow inside, and from Root to Crown envision the image of the Milky Way inside that vast inner space – and in the midst of that Comity of Stars, behold the Seven Great Stars shining brightly, with three Great Luminous Channel-Ways passing through the center of this image, one straight from Root to Crown like an arrow, and the two others crisscrossing at each Interior Star.

There, in your Holy Crown, is the Palace of Kali Imma – let your consciousness move through the three Channel-Ways by conscious intention, like a rushing fire and radiant holy breath, and passing through the Interior Stars envision that by the Divine Mother's will and the grace of her Holy Child you magically appear in their Holy Palace of Lights.

Her Palace is as a Sevenfold Star with Seven Gates, and at each of the Gates of Light is a Holy Archangel – within this is the Image of the Mother and Child and their Great Luminous Assemble; they are seated in the Center of Four Great Pillar-Angels, with a canopy formed by a Great Ofan, assuming the appearance of the starry night sky – beyond is the Great Void of Ain.

With the intonation of Ah give offering of your light-power to Kali Imma and her Holy Son, and worship in the Shekinah of El Elyon, offering up prayers for all creation. (This offering is light going up from your Heart Star to your Holy Crown Star, directed to them by conscious intention.)

As they receive your offering behold their glory growing brilliant and see them smiling upon you and blessing you with light-streams from their bodies and light-vestures; a blessings of rainbow light, dark radiance and white brilliance – all blessings of the Supernal Light-presence and Light-power.

Take up the holy chant: Ki-Ah-La-Yo, Yo-Ma-Ma-Yo, Ah-Yah-Ma, Ah-Yah-Ma, Ah-Yah-Ma; as you chant this envision her Holy Child dissolving into fluid flowing light, that Divine Light becoming stream of Holy Light gather at your Crown, and pouring down into your Heart.

Then take up the holy chant: Ki-Ah-La-Ya, Sho-Ma-Sha, Ma-Sa-Yah, Yo-Ah, Yo-Ah, Yo-Ah; with this chant focus on your Brow Star, envisioning the Sun of White Brilliance shining there – this causing all Holy Stars to shine with unimaginable brilliance and making your Body of Light radiant with Rainbow Glory.

Now intone IAO-OAI, and as you do envision that you dissolve into fluid flowing Rainbow Light and pour into the Sacred Heart-Womb of Kali Imma, merging with her as her Holy Child, Kali Shemesh.

Then, as the Divine Mother, intone: Ha-Yah-Ah, and like a rainbow in the sky dissolve into the Clear Light Ground, you and your entire Palace of Light;

From within this Womb of Emptiness, all magically arises once again as before, the Holy Mother and Child, the Palace and you in Jeweled Light Body; taking up the chant, Yah-Ma-Ma- Yah Yah-O-Way, remember all living spirits and souls within the countless realms, worlds and universes of the Entirety, and envision the Divine Light of the Supernal Shekinah pouring out upon them, beholding this Fiery Light making all like unto itself, enlightening and liberating all spirits and souls as in the End-Of-Days, the Apocalypse.

Then with a sharp intonement, say: Peh-Peh-Peh, Amen, seeing all restored, sacred as it is, all blessed by Kali Imma and her Holy Child.

When this is accomplished, take up the holy chant, Sha-Ma-Sha, Ka-Ah-La-Yah, and envision you dissolve once again into fluid flowing light and shoot into the Sacred Heart of Kali Shemesh, merging completely with the Holy Child of Kali Imma – abide in this Holy Union as long as you can.

When the mind moves and you are in your apparent physical body again, envision the Divine Light descending from above and passing down into this Good Earth – and pray for this Good Earth and all beings to be gathered up in the Great Resurrection and Ascension; giving praise and thanks to the Dark Mother and her Holy Child, and to the Supreme, dedicate the merit of your meditation to all beings, and offer it up as glorification of the Supreme and the Shekinah of the Supreme.

When all is accomplished and you go out into the world, go as the Holy Child of Ma, and in all that you do know that you are the Child of Ma playing in her lap –

all as She wishes.

Live as the Child of Ma, honoring her always and in everything.

This is the Way of Union with the Black Madonna and Holy Child.

*When initiates wish to extend the duration of this practice they will use a rosary consecrated to Ma and count their chants with it - a full round of the rosary for each chant. (This rosary may be kept in the shrine or it may be worn, all as inspired by the love of Ma.)

The opening of instructions in this practice is given in the traditional way – there is always something of a playful spirit when they are spoken, and one must entertain a playful contemplation to penetrate the symbolism of what is said, both in introduction and in the outline of the practice itself.

May the blessings of Ma be upon one and all alike; may all who desire it receive the Chrism of the Supernal Shekinah – Amen.

Mystery of the Crucifixion

According to the Acts of John when Master Yeshua was on the cross at a certain point John was overcome be grief at the sight of the Master's suffering and fled to the Mount of Olives, entering into a cave. There, while the crucifixion was underway, Christ appeared to him and revealed the Mystery of the Cross, imparting the inmost level of Gnostic and Light Transmission to his beloved disciple. As the mystery is spoken in the Acts of John, so also is it spoken among us, for it is a divine vision that has transpired in the experience of many adepts and masters of the tradition who have sought the knowledge, understanding and wisdom of the Holy Cross.

This is a mystery the runs deep, for the purpose of the crucifixion is the revelation of the Pleroma of Light in the Risen Christ, and yet the holy sacrifice of the Christ-bearer on the cross is as a ransoming of souls from realms of the archons and a purchasing of others from their bondage to the dominion of the demiurgos; hence, a great magical act dispelling the negative karma ("sin") of those who cleave to the Risen Savior. Although Gnostics do not believe in a collective and vicarious salvation, as taught in the atonement theology of orthodoxy, nevertheless we know and understand the liberative power of the crucifixion, for by it we behold the illusory nature of the reality that appears; specifically, the illusory nature of our bondage, sin and death. When this Divine Gnosis is acquired – when the Divine Illumination of the Risen Christ dawns, we are, indeed, "saved by the power of the cross," the "power of the blood of Christ." As it is taught in the Gnostic Gospel, "Do not despise the lamb, for by it you see the door."

Indeed, Gnostics do not believe in a collective and vicarious salvation through "blind belief," but rather we believe in the enlightenment and liberation of the soul through Divine Gnosis. This salvation, however, is universal, for the whole of Nature (Sophia Zoe) labors towards it and eventually all holy sparks will be gathered into the Mystical Body of the Risen Christ, all living spirits and souls reintegrated to the Light Realm. The Christ-bearer on the cross has become the vehicle of this great liberation within the Entirety, for through the appearance of death and resurrection the Divine Revelation of Christ is made complete – the power of the demiurge (cosmic ignorance) is dispelled and the True Light is made manifest; the Spirit of Truth made known to all who desire to listen and hear, and look and see.

As it has transpired in this world, so it is transpiring in all realms, worlds and universes of the Entirety, and so it continues to transpire among us – the Light-bearers enter, taking up their cross of incarnation to illuminate, heal and bring peace, laboring in the fields of sentient existence for the sake of the harvest of souls. Of this ongoing labor of the Great Liberation we shall say: It is the Continuum of Light Transmission imparted by the Gnostic Revealer that illuminates, heals and gives peace; receiving the Light from above we too become Lightbearers, Healers and Peacemakers, for the Master has said to us: "Take up your cross and follow me."

No one can reveal the Mystery of the Crucifixion to another, but rather it is the Light-presence (Christ) and Light-power (Holy Spirit) that reveals it – the Mother's Force, Divine Grace. Thus, if you seek to know and understand this great mystery you must pray and meditate upon it, and seek direct spiritual and mystical experience of it – calling upon the Divine Presence and Power of Christ to reveal it to you.

Yet, we can say this: The mystery is symbolized in the traditional robe of our Holy Order – the white robe represents the True Light that illuminates us, and the red cross and cincture is the power in the Blood of the Lamb that liberates us. Of the Body and Blood of the Lamb of God we can say: "The Body is Light; the Blood is Fire – this is the truth of the Human One of Light, the Divine I Am." Let the Templar contemplate and meditate upon the symbolism of their robe and upon the truth of the Mystical Body of the Risen Christ, seeking knowledge, understanding and wisdom through Divine Grace.

Here we must also say this: We do not worship a cross of wood, nor do we worship blood and flesh, but rather the symbol of our worship is the Cross of Light – we worship El Elyon (God

Most High) in the Light-presence and Light-power revealed in the Risen Christ (Christ Melchizedek).

Contemplative Meditation:

Read and contemplate the Revelation of the Mystery of the Cross in the Acts of John; when it is well known to you, then meditate upon it. Envision yourself as St. John the Beloved in the cave, as though in the womb of the Holy Mother, and envision the Human One of Light appearing before you – the Living Yeshua speaking the mystery to you, imparting to you the Gnostic and Light Transmission of the True Cross, the Great Seth (Shin-Tau). When the revelation is complete, take up the chant: Ha-Yah-Yah-Ha Yah-Ha-Sha-Va-Ha, and envision the Living Yeshua dissolve into fluid flowing light and pour into your heart, illuminating you with the knowledge, understanding and wisdom of the Sacred Heart.

Then chant Hallelu Yah three times and say, Amen.

Giving & Receiving:

If you wish to know the Mystery of the Crucifixion, then take up your cross and generate the Sacred Heart of Love and Compassion – envisioning a Cross of Solar Light within your lightbody, practice Giving & Receiving. (The entire mystery is made known in this holy meditation – it is nothing more or less than this.)

Mystic Robe & Cross:

Envision yourself in subtle crystalline light-body standing in a pillar of brilliant white light, diamond-like light sparkling with rainbow hues, and within your light-body envision a red cross formed of ruby light – abiding in this way, meditate upon the Great Mystery. When your meditation is complete chant: Ah-Ha-Yah, and when your chant concludes envision yourself disappear light a rainbow in the sky. When your mind moves again, chant: Yah-Ha-Vah, with the conscious intention that all beings receive the blessing of the Light of the Cross.

To seal the practice chant: Ah-Da-Na-Yah, with praise and thanksgiving in your heart, and with the intention of dedicating the merit to all beings. *If a person is in need of liberation from negativity or dark forces, take up this visualization, putting on the mystic robe of light and the cross, and envision rays of ruby red light streaming out of the cross in your light-body upon the person in need – inwardly or outwardly, as appropriate in the moment, intone: Yah-Ha-Va Peh Peh Peh once, in remembrance of the truth of the Risen Christ and with the conscious intention of dispelling the shades and shadows. If a person is in need of a blessing or illumination, taking up this visualization envision the white brilliance rays out upon them, blessings them, and intone Ad-Da-Na-Yah, with the conscious intention of blessing, whether inwardly or outwardly as the circumstances determine.

Union of the Crucifixion:

Abide in Primordial Meditation – when it is time, envision yourself in light-body with the Spiritual Sun in your heart. Then, envision a ray of light shooting forth from your heart and magically appearing as the Christ-bearer on the Cross before you – there is radiant glory about him and light streams forth from the apertures in his face and his wounds, as though inwardly he is filled with Divine Light, and there is a Great Sphere of White Brilliance above the image of the Christ-bearer on the Cross. Open your mind and heart to the Christos, and commune in the Divine Presence and Power of Christ – praying for yourself and all beings to receive the blessings and empowerment that flows from the Holy Cross. As you commune in this way, envision that light streams out of the Divine Image, blessings you and all beings. When your prayers are complete, take up the chant: Adonai Yeshua, Yeshua Messiah, and envision that white brilliance descends into the Divine Image of the Christ-bearer on the Cross and that the image of the Christ-bearer on the Cross becomes brilliant; becoming dazzling brilliance, envision that the image dissolves into fluid flowing light that streams to form a Holy Star above your head – envision this Divine Light pours down into your heart and merges with it as you conclude the chant. Your mind becomes the Mind of Christ, your heart becomes the Sacred Heart of Christ and your body becomes the Mystic

Body of Christ – abide in the awareness of this union as long as you can. Then, when your mind is set in motion again, give praise and thanks to El Elyon, and dedicate the merit of the practice – when you go out into the world walk in the remembrance of the Human One of Light in you and the truth of the Human One of Light in all beings, walk in a sacred manner practicing the Blessing Way. This is the simple Union of the Crucifixion. *When this method is stabilized you can practice the Transference of Consciousness Method of the Union of the Crucifixion.

Transference of Consciousness:

This practice is the same through the cycle of prayer and communion – you pray for all beings as you commune in the presence of the Christos, desiring the fulfillment of all beings, their happiness.

Then let the Holy Desire to satisfy and fulfill all beings yourself arise in your heart – the Holy Desire to offer up yourself as a blessing upon all beings.

Take up the chant: Adonai Yeshua Messiah, and as you do envision that a ray of Divine Light streams forth from Christ on the Cross striking you in the heart, and that your light-body becomes dazzling brilliance – dissolving into fluid flowing light, envision that you pour into the Sacred Heart of Christ, merging with the Christ-bearer on the Cross.

As the Christ-bearer on the Cross envision that the Mount of the Skull is a great cosmic mountain and that countless sentient beings gather around it seeking the blessing and grace pouring out through you – above envision the holy ones and immortals of the Pleroma of Light, the Divine Order, and on a plane going out from the base of the cross envision all manner of faithful and elect who are in the Way, and below envision all manner of sentient beings not yet in the way, to include such beings as the minions of the Lion-faced Ruler, hungry ghosts and demons.

61

Let yourself as the Christ-bearer on the Cross be filled with unconditional love and compassion for all beings – burn deep with love and the yearning to set all beings free, aware of the plight of the ignorance binding sentient beings to the gilgulim and the need for their salvation; know their sorrow and suffering as you own, and wish that they might know your peace and joy in the Light-presence and Light-power. With this holy desire, offer yourself to them, take up the chant: Kodesh, kodesh, kodesh Yahweh Elohim Tzavaot.

As you chant on the cross, envision the Divine Light descending upon your from above, and envision it pouring out through you to all beings gathered around you – see streams of light flowing out of your body as it becomes dazzling light, and see all beings surrounding you become dazzling brilliant light, all self-radiant with glory.

Then, as you near the end of the chant, envision that the entire assembly of beings becomes fluid flowing light and that, dissolving, they all pour into your Sacred Heart as Christ on the Cross – all blessed and uplifted in you.

Now take up the chant: Abba – drawing out the "ah" sound at the end of Abba, and envision that you, as the Christ-bearer on the Cross, dissolve into fluid flowing light and ascend, merging with the white brilliance above, bring up all beings in ascension with you. Abide in the awareness of this union as long as you can.

When your mind is set in motion again, envision yourself magically arise in light-body as the Risen Christ – the Living Yeshua, and with the conscious intention of extending your peace and joy in the world, take up the chant: Eheieh, Hayyah Yeshua. As you chant envision light shining forth from you upon the whole world and all who are in it – and envision the world and all who are in it becoming radiant with Divine Light, as though the whole earth is uplifted into the Pleroma of Light.

Then, when you cease from chanting, if inspired, speak from Pure Being – the Divine I Am, speaking blessings upon individuals and the world, all as the Holy Spirit speaks with, in and through you.

Then, letting go of the Body of Vision, as you depart from the awareness of perfect union, give praise and thanks to El Elyon and pray for the fulfillment of all things – the Reception of the Holy Bride, Shekinah of Messiah, and pray for the continuance of the true Apostolic Succession of Light-bearers on earth until all is accomplished. In completion, dedicate the merit of the practice to all beings – this concludes the Transference of Consciousness Union of the Crucifixion.

*When this method is stabilized you can practice Union with the Sacred Tau.

Union with the Sacred Tau (Shin-Tau)

Meditate upon the Holy Letters Shin and Tau – envision a sphere of white brilliance in the center of your head, and within the sphere of white brilliance envision the letter Shin formed red flaming fire within a Tau formed of black fire. Let your mind rest upon this internal image as the object of your meditation – this alone can bring about the experience of Union with the Sacred Tau.

Going Beyond:

Generate the crystalline light-body with three centers – root, heart and brow (red, gold and white, respectively, and with the three channel-ways; then envision the Shin-Tau formation in the Brow Star.

Take up the chant: Sha-Yah-Na Ta-Oa-Vey, and envision the black fire of the Tau leaps up out the top of your head, shooting forth to magically become the image of Christ on the Cross on the top of your head, the base of the cross resting in your Brow Center. Thus, at the base of the cross there is a ruby red Shin within a center of white light, the Tau having become the image of the Cross above your head. (The image of Christ on the Cross is as before, with the Great Sphere of White Brilliance above the Christ-bearer on the Cross).

Now, take up the chant: Sha-Ka-Yah-Na Ma-Sa-Yah, and as you do envision that a ray of light shoots down from the image of Christ on the Cross striking the letter Shin, and envision that the letter Shin sends forth a ruby ray through the central channel down to the Root Star, activating the fiery light-power in the Root. Envision the ascent of the fiery light through the central channel and as it passes up through the Spiritual Sun in your heart envision the Sun blazing forth with many light rays; as it reaches your Brow Star envision that the fiery-light transforms the Shin into itself and see this fiery light shoot up into the Sacred Heart of Christ on the Cross.

Then, take up the chant: Ah-Ha-Yah Ani-Ain, with the Holy Desire of self-offering, and as your do, gather yourself into the Spiritual Sun in your heart, and into the fiery light in the central channel; let Root, Heart and Brow dissolve as you ascend as the Fiery Light into the Sacred Heart of Christ on the Cross – you become the Christ-bearer on the Cross.

The visualization of the Mount of the Skull and assembly of beings is as before, but as you bless them take up the chant: Yah-Ha-Va-Ha Ah-La-Ha-Yah-Ma, and envision the Fiery Light, along with the Diamond Light from above, streaming out of your Sacred Heart upon them.

When all is gathered into your Sacred Heart, then as before, merge with the Sphere of White Brilliance, but taking up the chant: Yah-Ha-Ah.

As in the previous union, envision that you arise as the emanation of the Risen Savior giving blessings, but with the chant: Ya-Ha-Va-Sha-Ha.

Then bring the practice to completion as before – this is the conclusion of Union with the Sacred Tau.

(These are the essential instructions for Union with the Sacred Tau.)

*These practices are an extension of the Continuum of Union with the Holy Master and therefore us the same integration practices as that continuum – in the extension of the continuum, however, there is a deepening of one's active service and actual self-offering whenever possible, grounding the Union of the Crucifixion.

May we be blessed and empowered to take up our Cross and follow in the Way;
Amen.

Holy Grail: A Templar Practice

The Grail and Dove Meditation is a practice from the Order of Knights Templars. Having a vow to guard the Grail and the Order of the Grail, quite naturally practices have been generated to explore the mystery of the Holy Grail – the Grail and Divine Meditation being among them.

Taking up this practice of self-purification and the generation of the Sacred Heart, let the Templar contemplate their holy vow in the context of their experience of the Grail and Dove, and let them pray for insight in to the mystery of the Grail, calling upon Our Lady and Our Lord for their blessing – their inspiration.

Beginning the continuum of practice on the new moon, let the Templar perform the Grail and Dove Meditation each day until the moon waxes full – then on the full moon let them perform the Union with Our Lady of Templars, bringing their contemplation of the Holy Vow and Grail to fruition in this meditation of self-empowerment. (This is a common continuum of self-empowerment used by honorary Templars who have not received actual dubbing – at the completion of the practice on the full moon with Our Lady of Templars they will ceremonially speak the vow and their word to keep it. While this does not replace actual dubbing, it does help form a link to the spiritual transmission that flows through our Holy Order, as actual Templar initiates frequently perform the same continuum of self- empowerment following their initiation into the Order.)

Alternatively, a similar continuum is often kept by Templar initiates in preparation for taking up other practices of the Order, such as Union with the Holy Master, using the Grail and Dove Meditation as a preliminary practice in preparation for taking up a new practice. According to the masters of the tradition it is a practice of "Opening the Way" and when used as such, a continuum with the practice is begun on the new moon and brought to fruition on the full moon – riding the astral tide.

Aside from its use in Opening the Way it is an excellent and powerful spiritual practice of the Order of Knights Templars in and of itself, and is generally known to all initiates of the Order, having been inspired by the reception of Pistis Sophia into the teachings of our lineage in previous generations.

Mystery of the Holy Grail:

Self-purification and Consecration

According to the Pistis Sophia the Savior is the Father in the form of a Dove, and in the tradition we know that the Holy Bride is the Holy Grail into which the Savior poured himself out, so that she also became anointed with the Supernal Light of God. Receiving the anointing of the Supernal Light, the Gift of the Fiery Intelligence, we also have become Christian, that is to say we have become Christ-like, and we labor for the Pleroma of Christhood.

At the outset of our entrance into the Way we consciously invite the Anointed and Holy Spirit into our lives, and we offer ourselves to the Lord – to the service of the Divine Will and Divine Kingdom on earth. Indeed, each and every day when we arise, before we go out into the world, we invite the Anointed and Holy Spirit into our lives, and we offer up that day unto the Lord if we are wise. Thus, like Enoch, we walk with the LORD, and our Lord and Savior walks with us, and it is good, for in so doing we will also be taken up in divine rapture.

To the degree we purify ourselves and consecrate our lives to the Lord, and seek to live according to the Truth and Light revealed in our experience, the Anointed and Holy Spirit indwells us, that is to say the Father in the form of the Dove indwells us. When we open ourselves and make ourselves sensitive to the Holy Spirit, we receive her as Light from above and she works with, in and through us to accomplish everything good and true. Indeed! As the Fiery Light of Supernal Grace she descends upon us and enters into us each and every day, progressively transforming us into the image and likeness of Christ, the Perfect Human Being. With a heartfelt prayer and conscious intention we invite the Anointed and Holy Spirit into our lives, yet it is through contemplation and meditation that we make the Anointed and Holy Spirit welcome, and let the Light fully enter into us and penetrate and pervade the whole of our mind, heart and body.

Thus, along with our prayers a conscious intention, contemplation and meditation are also necessary in the Divine Life.

The Meditation of the Grail and Dove is one of the ways the masters of the tradition have generated to help us experience the Divine presence and power in full and to let it pervade our who mind, heart and body. It is a practice of selfpurification and of self-consecration, and many wonders have transpired for those who have practiced it. Thus, here we record it for our companions and for future generations of aspirants in the Christian mysteries.

The Holy Meditation:

Perform the Kabbalistic Cross and then abide in Meditation.

Then, envision your body as made of most subtle light and as though hollow; the surface image alone appearing with empty space within it, as though it is made of crystal that is subtly self-luminous. At your heart center envision the image of the Grail hovering there, formed of translucent golden light. Envision that this image of yourself stands on clouds and that there is a crystal clear blue sky above – let the sublime beauty of this image fill you with holy awe and wonder.

Holding this image in your mind let the conscious intention arise in your mind to receive the Holy Spirit, this becoming as an invocation. With the sound Ah, consciously open your mind, heart and life to the Holy Spirit, and yearn for her, focusing up above your head – continue to intone Ah with this holy aspiration.

Then envision a Dove of Light magically appearing in the sky above you, shining brighter than the sun – a Dove of White Brilliance, which is a diamond-like light sparkling with rainbow glory. With the sound Ha, consciously let your yearnings deepen and let them consume you utterly, as though the fire of Divine

Passion – continue to intone Ha with this holy desire.

Envision the Dove becoming a great stream of diamond-like light pouring down upon you, descending through the top of your head and streaming down into the Grail at your heart center – a stream about the thickness of a straw, completely radiant clear light sparkling with rainbow hues. Receiving this Light from above intone Yah, and as you continue to intone Yah see this light fill the Grail and the Grail overflow, and see the light pour down to your feet and rise up as though your body is being completely filled with this fluid of diamond-like light, just as the Grail is filled and overflowing with it.

Envision the Grail magically transforming into the image of the Spiritual Sun and your whole body filled with this "White Brilliance" which is diamond-like light, and see rainbows rays streaming from your body. As you envision this Body of Glory intone Ah-Ha-Yah (Eheieh: I am), merging yourself completely with the soundvibration, as with this Light-presence of the Father in the form of a Dove (the Anointed and Holy Spirit). Let yourself feel the subtle and sublime joy filling you and the profound peace of the Lord pervading you – when you fall into silence abide at-one with the Anointed and Holy Spirit.

Now envision the Good Earth below, and countless beings gather upon the earth below, as well as in the sky and above (countless beings in all directions of endless space); all gathered to receive the blessing of the Risen Savior. Intone Yahweh (or alternatively IAO), with the conscious intention that all beings be blessed and envisioning rainbow rays streaming out to them.

Then, continuing to envision the streams of blessings flowing out to all beings intone Yeshua (or alternatively Yahweh Elohenu), with the conscious intention for all beings to be liberated from negativity and darkness, and healed of all illness and dis-ease.

Then, intone El Shaddai, envisioning all beings radiant with Light and Glory as you are radiant with Light and Glory as the Risen Savior, holding the conscious intention of the Divine Illumination of all living spirits and souls.

Then, envision all beings joining with you as you intone Adonai, and worshipping God in Spirit and Truth with you. As they intone with you, see them dissolve into fluid flowing light and pouring into your Body of Glory, until all is gathered into you, as into the only begotten Sun of God.

Once all is gathered in, envision the Father in the form of the Dove, and as you intone Eheieh (standard intonement) envision yourself dissolving into fluid flowing light and shooting upward into the Dove of Light – when you fall silent abide in this Perfect Repose as long as you can.

Close with prayer and praise and thanksgiving, and then perform the Kabbalistic Cross. This is the Meditation of the Holy Grail and Dove of Light – also called the Meditation of All-Joy.

This is a delightful meditation that can be practiced at any time, whenever an initiate seeks to purify and consecrate her or himself to the Lord, or any time she or he seeks a deeper gnosis and communion with the Risen Savior and Holy Spirit. In the case of some initiates it has become their Heart-Practice. This is an inner practice generally given to experienced initiates, though under certain circumstances elders and tau may choose to teach it to novice initiates whom they believe might be able to perform it. This practice is powerfull, and some adepts have used it as an extension of their practice – arising in the Jeweled Body they then enact this Holy Mediation, within which is Gnosis of the Mystery of the Resurrection and Ascension.

Secret union with Our Lady

Our Lady of Templars is St. Mirya of Magdala as the High
Priestess of the Divine Order, she who dubs Templars of the Holy
Grail in the Rite of the Gnostic Mass and she who is Mother of the
Royal Blood, Mother of the Gnostic Apostolic Succession; Lord
Yeshua is the Master of our Holy Order and Lady Mirya is the
Mistress of our Order, which stands in guardianship of the Order
of Melchizedek. If you seek to make a heart offering to Our Lady
and to receive her blessing, the following is a practice of union
with her that will fulfill your desire.

*In all things let the Templar bring honor and glory to Our Lady.

Meditation:

Sit and abide, gathering yourself into the Spiritual Sun in your
heart, and pray to the Holy Mother that she might bless you…

Then see the image of the Holy Mother enthroned, with her Holy
Child in her arms on her lap, magically appear in the space before
you – radiant with heavenly glory.

Visualization:

She appears robed in red, with an inner robe of blue trimmed in
gold, and wears a veil and a crown, with sapphires in her crown;
her Son has an outer robe of gold and an inner robe of white, with
holy symbols on it in orange – he is as though six or eight years
old, the Eternal Youth. Their bodies are as though composed of
sunlight and this entire image is formed of translucent light, like a
rainbow in the sky.

On either side of the throne there are kerubim, male and female
with youthful faces, having four wings each – it is as though the
Mother with her Holy Child is the living ark of covenant in
the holy of holies.

Let your mind and heart open to her, and take up her chant: Ah Ya Imma Shekinah Ha- Messiah. (Before taking up the chant, if inspired, you may continue praying to the Holy Mother, or you may give praise and thanksgiving to her, worshipping before God the Mother, and then let the chant flow out of your devotion.)

As you chant, envision the Mother and Child smiling upon you, their light and glory streaming forth to bless you, your own body becoming luminous with their blessings and grace; as you near the end of the chant, envision the Mother's heart center shining like a brilliant star, and a ray shooting forth, striking your heart center, opening it completely.

From the Spiritual Sun in your heart envision a ray shooting forth, magically generating the glorious image of Our Lady or Templars before you.

Visualization:

She appears as a most beautiful and elegant woman, in the robes of a Holy Priestess-Queen, royal purple trimmed in gold, wearing golden ornaments with jewels of all colors in them and a crown studded with diamonds; she appears as though she is sixteen years old and she is bearing the Great Sword of the Gnostic Templars. As with the Mother and Child, she too is formed of the most subtle translucent light and her body shines with heavenly radiance.

With the appearance of Our Lady a great luminous assembly of holy ones and angels magically appears in the space surrounding her and you – the Royal Court of the Divine Order.

Envision her give salutations to the Holy Mother and Child, and then turn towards you – as she stands before you, with hands of light reach into your light-body and draw forth your heart center in the form of an envision emerald grail of light. Offer up this grail as yourself to Our Lady, and as you do see her bring the sword into union with the grail – the grail seeming to be filled with sunlight. Then envision her enacting the gesture of dubbing a Knight Templar with her sword; touching your head, your right shoulder and your left shoulder, and then touching your heart center – feel the fiery light of the Shekinah of Messiah fill you as she does this, and restore the grail to the sanctuary of your heart, receiving her blessing in full.

Now take up her holy chant: Ah Ya Ha Kallah Shekinah Ha-Messiah

As you chant this chant see the luminous assembly magically dissolve into the image of Our Lady and envision the image of our Lady become brilliant like a great star before you, and see her image condense into a light-seed of even more intense brilliance and shoot into your heart center. Then, in the same way, envision your light-body becoming like a brilliant star and condensing into a light-seed, and shooting into the Sacred Heart of the Holy Mother – as the Holy Mother with Child, envision that you dissolve into the Clear Light Ground, like a rainbow disappearing in the sky!

Abide in the Union of Clear Light as long as you can, but when you arise from it take up the chant of union: Ya Ha Imma Kallah Shekinah Ha-Messiah, and worship in the presence of Our Lady, aware of her presence manifest as you and entire reality display of your experience.

At the conclusion set the Holy Seal upon your practice, and then abide and ground the energy. This concludes the practice of Secret union with Our Lady.

*As you walk in the world remember and keep your holy vow, and view all that appears as her Palace, her Divine Body; hear all sound-vibration as the chant of union, her Divine Voice; and receive all thought and emotion arising in your mind as the innate wisdom display of her Divine Mind: this is the integration of the practice to daily living.

There is another version of this practice with Our Lady glad in ornamental armor, as a priestess-queen whose hosts are arrayed for battle. Also, there is a version of this practice taught in the Order of Mary, but rather than the dubbing of a Templar in that practice Our Lady receives the grail and places it in her heart center and she lays hands on the initiate – the rest, however, is just the same as what is given here.

May we be blessed to experience the Gnosis of Our Lady; amen.

Divine Guardianship

This practice may be performed in a ceremonial fashion, with the Templar drawing their sword, or it may be performed completely as an internal meditation, all as seems proper according to the need – essentially, this is a practice invoking divine guardianship of yourself, sacred space (or place) or someone else in need of protection against negative forces. If it is felt that a greater field of protection is necessary and the Templar elects to draw their sword for this invocation, then following the invocation the sword will be laid upon the altar (or on the floor before the altar) unsheathed for that day – then at the end of the day they will sheath the sword, saying, "It is accomplished, amen." Thus, the unsheathed sword becomes a physical talisman of a continuum of divine guardianship.

The Meditation/Ceremony:
Go within and abide in the sanctuary of your heart, envisioning the Spiritual Sun in your heart as the presence of the Lord seated there and gathering yourself into it; when you are centered within, envision a great sphere of light around you – white brilliance with an electric blue hue, and take up the chant: Yeshua Messiah; Kallah Messiah, abiding in the awareness of your innate unity with the Risen Messiah and Holy Shekinah.
(If the sword is to be drawn, it is drawn at this point.)
Then envision an emanation body arising from the Spiritual Sun in your heart in the image and likeness of Archangel Michael in Kerubic form – it is as though this emanation expands and you are in the midst of a great translucent light-body of the archangel, the emanation radiating from the Spiritual Sun in your heart. In other words, it does not manifest before you, but emanates from within and appears around you; it is as though your body of light expands, "growing" into the Great Angel.

The Visualization of Michael in Kerubic Form:

Archangel Michael appears clad in the garb of a warrior, having the body of a human being, but the four faces of the Kerub – face of a human, face of a lion, face of an eagle and face of an ox, each pointing to the four directions. The head is as though hollow, but filled with brilliant light that shoots forth from the apertures of the faces, as something like a lightening flash, and the head rotates this way and that, so that the faces change their direction in an uncanny and unsettling way – not human. In this form Michael has four great wings, and bears a sword of flashing fire and a round shield, as though made of moon-light with a cross of golden solar light on it. *The sword is not drawn at the outset of this visualization for the purpose of this practice. (In this meditation you arise in this form of Archangel Michael – it is *you* who appear like this.)

From the image of yourself as Archangel Michael, as though from the Light-presence within your angelic body, envision four images of yourself emanating from your heart center into the four directions – images that look exactly the same, and they stand facing out. Then from each of these images of Michael envision ten emanations of the same form emerging, also facing outward, so that a great circle is formed by the ban of forty-four Michael Angels, forty-five counting you.

Just as the Kerubic head of yourself as Michael rotates and spins, shifting the faces this way and that, so also do the heads of the entire assembly of Michael Angels, producing a thunderous vibration within spirit-space; in the midst of this, as Archangel Michael, take up the chant: Yahweh Elohim Tzavaot, hearing all of the Michael Angels of your emanated host take up the chant with you. As this chant resounds envision brilliant light shooting forth from all of the kerubic faces of yourself as Archangel Michael and your emanated host – a raying out into all directions of limitless space, purifying infinite space in all directions of all negative forces.

When this is accomplished, then take up the chant: Ya Mi Ha Michael with your emanated hosts, envisioning yourself as Archangel Michael drawing your sword of flashing fire and all of your emanated hosts drawing their swords – all together bringing the sword to the position of salute and then to a position on guard, ready to strike.

(If there is any specific dark and hostile force to be dealt with, as you arise in the kerubic form of Archangel Michael, it may be called by name, envisioned, and then struck by the power of your wings or struck by the flashing fire of your sword, all as is necessary to subjugate, banish or destroy. A dark and hostile force may be swiftly dealt with in this way simply by conscious intention and envisioned gesture, all in the remembrance of the Blessed Name [Yeshua Messiah], the Risen Messiah. A "strike with wings" is accompanied by the intonement of "Ya" and a "strike with sword" is accompanied by the intonement of "Ha.")

When the theurgic action is completed, envision the forty emanations of Michael Angels dissolving into the four emanated Michael Angels, then envision the four dissolving into fluid light and pouring back into your heart center as Archangel Michael; then, envision yourself, as Archangel Michael dissolving into fluid light and pouring back into your hearts center – the light gathered on top of your head and pouring down into your heart.

Centered in the Spiritual Sun within the sanctuary of your heart, and seeing the sphere of Divine Light surrounding you, take up the chant: Adonai Yeshua; Yeshua Messiah, aware of yourself inseparable from the Mystical Body of the Risen Messiah.

When you fall silent, completing the chant of the Blessed Name, abide in union with the Lightpresence and Light-power of the Anointed.

Close with praise and thanksgiving to El Elyon, Christ the Logos and Christ the Sophia, and in remembrance of the blessing Melchizedek spoke upon Abram when he returned from the battle with the kings of Edom; then place the Holy Seal on the practice, praying for blessings and grace to pour out upon all beings, and the dedication of merit to all beings. This concludes the practice of invoking the kerubic form of Archangel Michael for divine guardianship.

If this is to be practiced for another person in need of divine guardianship, the image of that person in light-body may be drawn into the sacred circle once the full emanation is complete – their light-body being envision within your emanation body manifest as Archangel Michael; conversely, you may also emanate a light-body in the form of Archangel Michael and envision that you go to the person, performing this practice in the subtle dimension of their own space – either way it is modified, the practice remains basically the same. It may also be performed for an entire circle, community or group of people by envisioning them in light-bodies within the sacred circle, and again, the practice remains basically the same.

(This practice may also be used as a general method of self-purification.)

In such theurgic practices at no time should a human person ever be the object of focus, but rather any "strike" must be focused against the negative forces within and behind a person – for as it is written, "…our battle is not with blood and flesh…"
This practice can be used to defend against assaults of dark and hostile forces, and likewise to banish dark and hostile forces from a place; however it is not used as an "exorcism" of negative forces "possessing" a person, but rather other methods are used for that purpose by Templar initiates.

As mentioned at the outset, a ceremonial version of this practice can be done in which the Templar draws her or his sword, though most often we find that is not necessary, as this is a very powerful and effective practice apart from any outward gesture. According to the tradition, a master of the art does not need to draw their sword to accomplish anything, but rather can accomplish everything by a simple conscious intention, all in the Grace of the

Risen Messiah. This well speaks our noble ideal as Templars of the Holy Grail.

In more extreme circumstances there is a similar practice that invokes the Archangel Kamael, likewise there is a practice invoking the wrathful emanation of Kamael, the "Lord of the Wrathful Palace" as well as the "Four Great Wrathful Guardians" and "Twenty-Two Wrathful Guardians" of the Palace.

May we be empowered as guardians of the Grail and the Order of the Grail; may the Continuum of Light Transmission remain present with us until all is accomplished –
amen.

Divine Guardianship: Secret work with Kamael

Michael is called the "commander of the celestial hosts," but Kamael is called the "champion of God," the great guardian of the assembly of the faithful and elect. Kamael presides over the order of the Seraphim, which is the order of angels said to enter and abide in the inmost presence of God; thus Kamael presides over the hosts that serves as the "royal guard" of the Divine Order. Therefore Archangel Kamael is invoked by Templars when there is a need for greater guardianship and purification, or when confronting very powerful dark and hostile forces. However, as Kamael is the manifestation of Gevurah (Severity, Rigor or Judgment) at the level of Beriyah, traditionally a Templar will enact some form of self-purification before invoking Kamael, "the burner of God" or "fire of God," for Kamael is an intense archangelic presence that reflects the karmic continuum of those to whom he appears. Thus a cycle of self-purification and banishing is taken up by Templars as part of the continuum invoking Kamael, and they look to see that they are honoring their vow and walking in a sacred manner before invoking him. Like the invocation of Archangel Michael for divine protection, the invocation of Kamael can be performed as a meditation or as a ceremonial gesture, thus, just as with the invocation of Michael the sword of the Templar may be drawn and used as a physical talisman of the continuum of guardianship. Likewise, on some occasions the Templar's altar may be draped in red cloth and five red candles may be placed on the altar, and in place of the cross a pentagram might be put on the altar for an invocation of Archangel Kamael – when this is done the altar is left in this way for three days and each day the invocation of Kamael is performed.

The Rite of Invocation:

At the outset a banishing ceremony is performed, manifesting the sacred circle. (This may be accomplished inwardly through visualization of light-body emanation if the invocation is to be performed as a meditation – all ceremonies can be performed as meditations in this way.)

Then the Templar abides in prayer, preparing her or himself for the invocation (psalms or other scriptures may be chosen to be read).

When the Templar is ready, they envision their body as though formed of transparent crystal, with empty space inside and with the Spiritual Sun shining in the place of the heart; on the surface of the body they envision a subtle fire or energy in free motion, and they envision a great sphere of flaming fire surrounding them – this light and fire dispel all inner negativity as the Templar takes up the chant: Adonai Yeshua; Shekinah Ha-Messiah, aware of their innate union with the Holy Lamb of the Apocalypse.
Then, in the same way as in the invocation of Michael for divine guardianship, the Templar emanates as the Archangel Kamael – but a focused force of emanation is envisioned up through the top of the head, like a solar flare bursting forth from the Spiritual Sun in the heart.

Visualization of St. Kamael:

Kamael is a fierce and fiery presence, appearing in human form, glad in what appears like bronze armor, bearing a sword and a spear – the sword is flashing fire, like a bolt of lightening held in his hand, and the spear is a rod of unquenchable fire; there is a plume of flames coming out the top of his helmet and the visor of the helmet is down concealing his awesome and dread countenance, but hints of a fiery light shine from within. He has two great and powerful wings, with celestial fire shooting through them, and rides upon a seraf in the form of a great fiery winged serpent (dragon). There is an awesome and terrible aura of flames about him, such as no evil spirit can endure. Kamael has no sheath for his sword, for he is "pure judgment before which no evil can stand."

Arising as Archangel Kamael the Templar is aware of her or himself as "fire consuming fire," the Shekinah of the Holy One as a "Man of War," and from that fire in their heart they envision four great serafim emanating to the four directions in the form of fiery winged serpents (dragons) facing outward. With the

81

emanation of the four serafim they envision a great circle of flames spontaneously appearing – it is a "vision of judgment," all manifest is the most subtle translucent light.

(Above the Templar arising in emanation body as Archangel Kamael, in the advanced practice there is a visualization of the Holy Lamb of the Apocalypse, enthroned on the Book of Seven Seals, held on the lap of the Holy Mother – she wearing an outer robe of black and an inner robe of crimson red, with a veil over her head and a golden crown on the veil with a great ruby in the center of it. This image is envisioned as spontaneously appearing as though from "thin air.")

As Kamael, with five serafim, the Templar takes up the chant: Elohim Givor; Ish MiYLCHaMaH; DaYYan (Mighty God; Man of War; Judge)

As the Templar chants they envision the radiance of light and fire increasing within and all around, and flames of fire shooting forth, like vast solar flares, into all directions of infinite space – fire consuming all that is not like unto itself, devouring all negative forces that it touches, incinerating whatever it touches in an instant.

Then, as Archangel Kamael with hosts, the Templar takes up the traditional chant of Kamael: Ha Ka Yo Ma Sa Ka Ma El. (Alternatively, the outer version of the chant could be used: Ah Ya Ko Ma Kamael.) With this chant the Templar envisions bursts of fiery light going out into all directions of endless space, like spherical waves of fiery light, but in rapid succession – the pace increasing with the continued chant until there is one great flow of fiery light filling endless space. At the same time, lightening is envisioned flashing forth from the sword, striking any shade or shadow directly.

(In emanation body as Kamael a dark and hostile force may be struck with the power of the wings, sword, spear or gaze of the Great Angel; likewise they may be struck by the power of the gaze, breath, wings, claws, or tail of the holy serafim. Striking with wings the Templar intones "Ha," striking with sword they intone "Ka," striking with spear they intone "Yo," and striking with gaze they intone "Sa.")

When all is accomplished, endless space being purified of all negative forces, the Templar envisions the circle of fire dissolving into the four great serafim, and the four serafim dissolving and pouring back into their own heart center as Archangel Kamael; then they envision their emanation body of Kamael dissolving and pouring into the heart center of their transparent light-body. Then the Templar takes up the chant: Yeheshuah-Yehovosha, aware of their innate union with the Risen Messiah and entering union at the fruition of the chant.

(In the advanced practice, at this point, the Templar performs a transfer of consciousness, envisioning the dissolution of their aura of flames into the transparent light-body and gathering their consciousness into the Spiritual Sun at the Heart, then envisioning the Star Center shooting up out of the top of the head into the image of the Holy Lamb above. When the transference of consciousness is complete, as the Holy Lamb of the Apocalypse, the Templar envisions her or himself dissolving into the Clear Light Ground, disappearing like a rainbow in the sky! This is called "supreme purity" and is perfect peace – repose.)

When the movement is complete, the Templar gives praise and thanksgiving to El Elyon, and to the Virgin Mother and the Holy Lamb, and remembers the blessing that Melchizedek spoke upon Abram when he returned from his battle with the kings of Edom; then the Templar places the Holy Seal on the rite, dedicating the merit. This concludes the practice of invoking Archangel Kamael for divine guardianship.

(This practice of Kamael is extended as invisible spiritual assistance to others in the same way as the practice of Michael.)

If one studies and contemplates the invocations for "divine guardianship" with Michael and Kamael one will find that they have a deep mystical intention, as well as their stated theurgic intention, for they are practices of *self-purification and union* that are frequently used as daily practices by Templars in their Self-realization process. Typically, first a new Templar initiate will learn the practice with Michael, and once skill is gained with that practice they will take up the practice with Kamael, then, perhaps, they may take up the practice of Kamael in wrathful emanation – the three representing cycles of self-purification, each more intensive than the other.

Templar Eucharist Ceremony-Meditation

The celebration of the Wedding Feast is a central practice of Templars , for within the wedding feast is the mystery of the Holy Grail and the Order of the Grail, of which Templars are sworn guardians – the bread is Logos and the wine is Sophia, and in their union there is Life and Light, the Christos. Thus, partaking of the wedding feast you become the Bridal Chamber, your subtle body being transformed into the Light and Fire of the Spiritual Sun of God, the True Light of El Elyon.

The Rite of Wedding Feast:

Let the Templar lay out bread and wine in remembrance of the priest-king Melchizedek who brought forth bread and wine to Abram and Sarai when they returned from their battle with the Kings of Edom; and having laid out bread and wine, let the Templar contemplate the mystery of this Rite of Melchizedek performed by the Master of our Holy Order as the "Last Supper" – an ancient Rite of the Holy Grail.

(The Sword of the Templar is laid in front of the altar, sheathed at the outset.)

Then let the Templar light the candles on the altar and kindle incense, giving praise and thanks to El Elyon and to the Divine Order, remembering the Gnostic and Light Transmission manifest among us through the Risen Christ and all of the Light- bearers who have walked among us – all of the tzaddikim (holy ones) and maggidim (angels) of the Communion.

Taking up the sword, unsheathing it, and holding the sword before her or himself in the position of salutation, let the Templar contemplate the words of the Master to his disciples when he inquired of them, "Do you have a sword among you?" before his death and resurrection, and his response when they answered saying, "Yes, Adonai, we have one among us," and he said to them, "Good, that is enough."

Remembering the sword in their hands as this Holy Sword, the Sword of Wisdom, the Sword of Truth – let the Templar call upon the Maggid of the Sword to dwell in its Emanation Body (the sword), saying:

O Great Angel of the Sword, Mighty Kerub, come now into your Emanation Body, driving out all evil and darkness, dispelling all shades and shadows – purifying endless space of all obstructions to the Light of the True Cross (Shin Tau).

Let the Templar envision an aura of fiery light about the sword, the blade of the sword becoming like a lightening bolt – and let them proclaim: "Be gone, O evil spirits; be banished, O shades and shadows – Behold the flashing fire of the sword of the Great Kerub driving you out of the people and the land!" As this is said, let the Templar envision flashing fire going out from the sword into all directions of endless space, purifying all shades and shadows from internally appearing space and externally appearing space just the same – holding the awareness of all that arises and appears as the radiant display of mind, the awareness of the ain nature of mind and the ain nature all that appears.

Then let the Templar intone the divine name Agla and circumambulating let the Templar chant Atoh Givor Leolam Adonai, manifesting the Sacred Circle – returning to the East let the Templar proclaim: "You are heroic for the world, O Lord!" With sword in hand, let the Templar call upon the Name of the LORD, intoning:

Baruch Ha-Shem
El Elyon, Eheieh (Ah-Ha-Yah), Yahweh (Yah-U-Ah), El Shaddai, Adonai
Yah, Yahweh Elohim El, Elohim Givor

Yahweh Tzavaot, Elohim Tzavaot Ararita
Holy One, Bornless One
Heavenly Father and Earthly Mother,
Spiritual Sun and Holy Spirit,
I praise you and give all glory to you, I praise and bless your Holy
Name, Let your Holy Shekinah rest upon me,
And fill this space with your Divine Light,
May you and your name be one on the face of the Earth, May the
Light of the True Cross shine forth in this world! Amen.

(As this invocation is spoken, let the Templar envision Divine
Light from above pouring down through the top of their head
into their heart, manifesting as the Spiritual Sun within the
sanctuary of their heart – their whole body becoming filled with
the Holy Light of the El Elyon, the Divine Most High, and a great
aura of Divine Light shining about them.)

Then, let the Templar trace a great cross of light over the altar – in
the form of a Celtic cross, intoning Abba-Imma while tracing the
vertical axis; and Yeshua Messiah while tracing the horizontal
axis; and Ruach Ha-Kodesh while tracing the circle in the middle.
Then let the Templar say, "Blessed are you Adonai, who brings
forth bread and wine, giving Light and Life to all who desire to
receive it; blessed are you, Adonai."

When this is accomplished, let the Templar invoke the Divine
Presence from the Four Direction, East, West, South and North, as
inspired.

East corresponds to the divine name of Yahweh, Archangel
Raphael, the Kerubic Face of the Human One, the place of dawn,
Light-bearers and Knowledge-keepers, the element air and power
of mental being;

West corresponds to the divine name of Eheieh, Archangel Gavriel, the Kerubic Face of the Eagle, the place of sunset, ancestors and wise ones, waters of reflection, Thunder Beings, the element water and power of vital-emotional being;

South corresponds to the divine name Elohim, Archangel Michael, the Kerubic Face of the Lion, the place of the blazing sun (noonday), martyrs and righteous warriors, the Path of the Milky Way, the element fire and power of the will and spiritual being; North corresponds to the divine name Adonai, Archangel Uriel, the Kerubic Face of the Ox, the place of the midnight sun, Cave of Machpelah, elder races and star people, the element earth and our physical being and life.

(With each invocation the Templar envisions the corresponding archangel magically appearing; until all four are present – the visualization can be as simple as four pillars of light: golden, blue, red and green, respectively.)

When this cycle of invocation is complete the Templar turns their sword down, and invokes the blessing of Metatron and Sandalfon, the height and depth; then she or he envisions the archangels dissolving into fluid light, the light of the archangels gathering over their head and pouring down into the Spiritual Sun in their heart. Then the Templar lays their sword in front of the altar unsheathed.

(At this point the Templar may remain standing or be seated, all as she or he likes.)

From the Spiritual Sun within the Templar's heart, let them envision a ray of light shoot forth, magically appearing as the image of the Holy Bride before them, bearing the Great Sword of the Templars – she appears robed in crimson, wearing golden ornamentations, including a golden crown with sky-blue topaz in it, as priestess-queen of the Divine Order.

There is a hint of an inner robe of white brilliance beneath her outer garment, and her crown sits on a crimson veil over her head – she is radiant with heavenly glory and her face shines with what seems like sunlight.

Along with Our Lady in Red a great luminous assembly of tzaddikim and maggidim appear – in remembrance of the Cosmic Christ they assume the forms of Light-bearers from the many lineages of the Divine Order that have manifest in the world and in other worlds. (This entire body of vision is formed of translucent light, like a rainbow in the sky.)

With hands of light (and a physical gesture of hands to the heart center) let the Templar reach into the sanctuary of their heart and envision drawing out their heart as a cup of emerald light, and offer this cup up before Our Lady – let them see her touch the top of their head with the sword, then their right and left shoulders, and then see her turn the sword downward bringing the tip of the sword into the grail of their heart. As she does this, let them envision the cup filled with golden and rainbow light, and then envision her removing the sword, and let the Templar envision themselves restoring the grail of their heart to its place – let the Templar feel the Divine Love of Our Lady and Our Lord fill them, the boundless compassion of the Messiah.

Now let the Templar envision Our Lady holding the sword before her inverted, the pommel to her brow, and let the Templar take up her blessing chant: Ah Yah Ha Ma, Kallah Messiah, Shekinah Ha-Messiah. As they chant, let the Templar envision her smiling upon them and her image growing brighter, and let them envision light streaming from her blessing them – their own light-body growing brighter and brighter. Then, let the Templar envision her dissolving into fluid flowing light, which gathers on top of their head, as though a crown of light, and then pours down into their heart as they bring the chant to cessation.

As this happens, let them envision the Spiritual Sun in the heart expanding to fill their whole body, and in an instant, as by magic, let them envision themselves transformed into the image of the Holy Master, the Risen Christ. (The luminous assembly does not dissolve at this point, but only the image of Our Lady dissolves.)

*The outer robe of the Master is violet light, the inner robe is white brilliance; his face shines like the sun and there is a great aura of rainbow glory about him.

Let them take up the chant of union: Ah Ha Yah Yeshua Messiah, with the conscious intention of a self-offering as a blessing upon all beings. Let the Templar envision rainbows rays of light streaming forth upon the luminous assembly – blessing all who are present as they chant; then, ceasing from the chant, as the Master, let them invite all beings to the Wedding Feast, that all who desire to receive the Spirit of Truth might partake and be blessed.

(If seated, the Templar will stand in this next cycle to go to the altar.)

Going to the altar and placing hands over the cup, as the Master let them say, "Ah Ha Yah – I Am, this is my blood poured out for you – it is Holy Fire, come and drink of it."

And placing their hands over the bread, as the Master let them say, "Ah Ha Yah – I Am, this is my body broken for you – it is Supernal Light, come and eat of it."

Then, as the Master, let the Templar break the bread, and taking a piece of the bread let them uplift the cup – intoning the divine name: IAO-OAI as they dip the bread into the cup, aware of the sacred unity within and behind all that appears, let them eat the bread and drink the wine on behalf of all living spirits and souls – all sentient beings held in the Sacred Heart of the Master, Our Lord.

(Having done this, let them envision the luminous assembly dissolving into fluid light and gathered as a single light, like a brilliant seed, let them envision it shooting straight into their heart.)

Then let the Templar, appearing as the Master, say, "Do this in the Holy Remembrance of the Divine I AM," and then let them intone: Ya Ha Sha Va Ha, Amin." ("Amin" is used for the purpose of intonement.)

Remaining in the Emanation Body of the Holy Master, let the Templar say, "The one who lives by the sword shall die by the sword."

Then, as the Master, let them pick up the sword and sheathe it, saying, "It is accomplished – let there be peace." Let them lay down the sword once this is done.

Then, let them say, "O children of the earth, remember yourselves as children of Light and receive my peace."

Then, as the Master, let them intone: Sha-Lom three times. Let them then dissolve the Emanation Body into the Spiritual Sun in their heart center and intone: Hallelu Yah three times, raising both arms up in a gesture of praise and salutation.

Let them place the Holy Seal on the ceremony with a Kabbalistic Cross and the dedication of merit, praying that all beings receive this blessing and grace; that all beings might be taken up in the Great Resurrection and Ascension. This concludes the practice of the Templar Wedding Feast.

*Once the bread and wine are consecrated, but before the breaking of the bread, this is a "theurgic window" in the rite when an initiate may speak from *Gnostic Being* and things will manifest as they are spoken, or during which brief theurgic works may be accomplished on behalf of others – all as the Templar is inspired by the Holy Spirit.

If there is any wine remaining, along with the bread, it is cast out upon the earth in a respectful place with prayers for the blessing of all beings. (If performed as a daily ritual an initiate can use red juice, such as pomegranate or cranberry juice, in place of wine if they desire.)

May we abide in the Holy Remembrance of Union – Divine Gnosis; amen.

Secret union with the Holy Master:

The Risen Christ, the Living Yeshua, is the Master of our Holy Order – there is no other; the essence of the Holy Master is Pure Radiant Awareness, nothing more and nothing less.

This is the Union of Mother and Daughter Sophia, the union of the primordial ground of Divine Mind, from which all arises, and the radiant display of all that appears; hence, the realization of all that appears as the radiant display of the One Mind of All – the One-Being Consciousness-Force, which has been called the Living Father.

According to the Gnostic gospel, the sign of the Living Father in us is "movement and repose": recognizing the nature of mind – Pure Radiant Awareness, though mind, consciousness or soul appears to move and arise as a radiant display, as in a dream, nevertheless one abides in repose, unmoved. This is the wakening of Christ in us – the bornless nature of the Human One of Light: Shin-Tau (the Great Seth), also called Melchizedek; King of Righteousness, King of Peace.

Abiding in the state of Pure Radiant Awareness (non-dual gnostic awareness) there is no meditation, for one abides in Truth Consciousness; the Templar takes up the practice of meditation to reintegrate their mind, consciousness or soul into this Light Continuum – Pure Radiant Awareness, but the Master of the Temple has no meditation, for that one abides as bornless being, Christ Melchizedek. So it is written, "If your heart runs, return it to the place."

Here we have spoken an open secret regarding the Grail and Order of the Grail, and we shall remind the Templar of their Holy Vow to guard it; for the one who abides in Pure Radiant Awareness is perfect in keeping the Holy Vow – all is accomplished.

The following is the Continuum of Union with the Holy Master:

Putting on the Name of the Lord – Purifying Obstructions
(Main Practice):

Let the Templar abide in Primordial Meditation, and let them
envision themselves in the clear crystalline light-body, and taking
up the chant: Yah Ah Ha Da Va Na Ha Yah, let them envision
the holy letters of the Tetragrammaton filling their light-body
(Yod, their head, first He their shoulders and arms, Vau their
torso and the final He their hips and legs; these letters appear as
fierce flaming fire, burning away all impurity in mind, speech and
body). It is as though the entire body becomes this Holy Fire and
all that is not this Holy Fire is burned utterly away in an instant.
Then let the Templar take up the chant: Ah Yah Da Ha Na Va Yah
Ha, and as they do this let them envision the holy letters of the
Great Name dissolving into one another, from the final He
to the Yod, leaving only a holy sparks of fiery light in the crown.
(These two chants are the unification of Yahweh with Adonai and
Adonai with Yahweh, respectively.)

Now let the Templar intone "Ah" three times and envision this
holy spark igniting and magically transforming into a spark of
intense white brilliance, a holy seed of diamond-like light, with
rainbow hues sparkling from it; then let them take up the chant:
Ah Yah Ha Ha Yah Va Ha Ha, and as they do this let them see a
ruby red ray, a sapphire blue ray, a golden ray and an emerald
ray shooting down into their transparent light-body, manifesting
as Yod-He- Vau-He, respectively, just as before, but now the holy
letters are formed of this jeweled translucent light. (Yod-Red; He-
Blue; Vau-Golden; He-Green)

Then, taking up the chant: Yah Ah Ha Ha Va Yah Ha Ha, let them
envision the dissolution of letters into one another as before – all
dissolving into the holy spark of diamond-like light, which now
shines even more intensely than before. (These two chants are
the unification of Eheieh with Yahweh and Yahweh with Eheieh,
respectively.)

Now let the Templar into "Sho" three times and envision the holy spark magically transforming into the shape letter Shin, but remaining diamond-like white brilliance; then taking up the chant: Yah Ha Sha Va Ha, let the Templar envision the Shin descending, as though by an invisible pathway to the place of their heart, their subtle light-body becoming filled with this diamond-like light, sparkling throughout with rainbow hues. Then, taking up the chant: Yah Ha Sha Va Ha Ma Sa Yah, let them envision the Shin transform into the image of the Spiritual Sun, and envision the orb of the Spiritual Sun expand to fill their whole subtle body of light, as though they emanate as the Human One of Light; and then let them envision their appearance magically transform into the Emanation Body of the Risen Christ – the body like sunlight, the inner robe white brilliance and outer robe of violet light, with a great aura of rainbow glory.

Abiding in this union with the Risen Christ – emanated as the Holy Master, let the Templar generated the Sacred Heart of Love and Compassion for all beings in the Entirety, and let them wish that all beings receive the blessing of Divine Grace, so that liberated from sorrow and suffering, established in peace and joy, all might be drawn up in the Great Resurrection and Ascension, Divine Rapture.

Then let them envision the entire world and all beings in it as though formed of translucent light, and intoning: Ah Da Na Yah, let them envision the entire radiant display dissolving into fluid flowing light and pour into their Emanation Body as the Risen Christ. Then, intoning: Yah Ha Va Ha, let them see their Emanation Body dissolve into the Spiritual Sun; and then intoning Ah Ha Yah Ha, let them envision the Spiritual Sun dissolving into the White Light Seed - intoning "Ah" three times let them dissolve themselves as the Light Seed into Clear Light, like a rainbow disappearing into the sky. This is called "No More Obstructions," and is it All-Good.

Let the Templar abide in this Holy Perfection as long as they can, but when they depart from it let them give praise and thanksgiving to El Elyon, and pray for all living spirits and souls, dedicating the merit of the practice for the benefit of all beings. This concludes the practice of "Putting on the Name of the Lord". Although Putting on the Name of the Lord is the preliminary practice for the Palace of the Risen Christ – the method of self-purification for the continuum of Union with the Risen Christ, nevertheless it is the main practice of the continuum of Union: the entire continuum of Union is in this meditation and, in truth, nothing more or less is needed. However, the Palace Meditation and other practices are generated to facilitate the full realization of Perfect Union. Likewise, they are generated as the noble gesture of the Sacred Heart extending blessings, grace and holy sanctuary to all beings, for though one might attain realization there are countless beings that remain in their bondage and the harvest of souls continues throughout the Great Aeon (great cosmic cycle).

Integrating Union into all Actions:
As the Templar walks in the world, let them walk in beauty and holiness as an Emanation of the Holy Master: all that outwardly appears are the Emanation Body and Palace of the Risen Christ; all sound if the manifestation of the Holy Chant, the Living Word; all thought and emotions arising in the mind are the innate display of the Master's Wisdom. Thus, the Templar never departs from Union with the Holy Master.

Dream Union:

When the Templar is going to sleep, let them envision the image of the Risen Christ above their head and let them gather their consciousness as the Spiritual Sun in their heart; then let them dissolve themselves as the Spiritual Sun into fluid light that flows up out the top of their head, merging with the Holy Master.

Alternatively, let the Templar envision him or herself as the Emanation Body of the Master; then let them envision the Emanation Body dissolving into the Spiritual Sun in their heart, and the Spiritual Sun dissolving into the White Light Seed at the top of the head; in fruition let them envision the Light Seed disappearing into the Clear Light – abiding in the Presence of Awareness joined to No-thingness (Ain).

Awakening Union:

When the Templar awakens in the morning, let them hear the trumpets of the holy maggidim, and let them hear the tzaddikim (holy ones) and maggidim (angels) chanting: Yah Ha Sha Va Ha Ma Sa Yah. Let them envision themselves spontaneously emanating as the Risen Christ; all that they do upon awakening let them do as the Holy Master.

May all living spirits and souls be taken up in the Great Resurrection and Ascension – joined to the Mystical Body of Christ may they realize Divine Rapture; amen.

The Practice of Taking Sanctuary of the Sacred Heart

Abide in Meditation and let your mind and heart become clear; then shift into contemplative meditation, drawing to mind the truth of the demiurge and archons and their dominion, allowing deep concern to arise for the plight of the mind or soul-stream bound to the dominion of the demiurge (cosmic ignorance) and the potentially endless cycles of transmigration throughout the Great Cosmic Aeon – especially the possibility of inauspicious incarnations. Contemplate the play of cosmic and spiritual forces, and the dampening field or psychic gravity generated by the vast array of negative forces and the great conflict of forces in this world, and look and see the need for the Holy Sanctuary of Grace and divine assistance in order for the mind or soul-stream to acquire the Divine Gnosis that illuminates and liberates – the need for the *Gnostic Revealer*.

Consider the good fortune of coming into contact with the Gnostic and Light Transmission in this life, and having the conditions necessary to take up the spiritual life and practice, and the grace of the Holy Spirit that has lead you to be received by your Root Tzaddik into the Light Transmission lineage; thus, let a strong desire to make the most of this present opportunity arise in your heart.

Recognizing your own plight of bondage to the dominion of the demiurge, contemplate the plight of the many peoples in this world – the billions and billions of sentient beings bound in this world and the immeasurable sorrow and suffering in this world, and the inevitability of ageing, illness, injury and death; and contemplate the infinite expanse of realms, worlds and universes of the Entirety and the countless sentient beings in them, all pervaded and bound up in the same sorrow and suffering.

Recall that even many great cosmic forces, gods and goddesses, and apparently fortunate individuals, remain in bondage, regardless of the illusory appearance of "good fortune"; and let the awareness dawn that only through the Sanctuary of Divine

Grace, and invisible assistance provided by the enlightened ones of the Divine Order, does the possibility of illumination and liberation of souls come into being – remember the virtue of authentic spiritual teachings and practices that open the way to Divine Gnosis.

With the awareness of the plight of all sentient beings in your heart, contemplate the need for the emanations of the Christ, the Gnostic Revealer, and the Apostles of Light in the realms, worlds and universes of the Entirety, and generate the holy desire to attain Divine Gnosis so that you might become a holy apostle of light bearing forth the Divine Light, Healing and Peace to all beings, serving in the harvest of souls, the Great Work.

Generating this awareness of faith, hope and love through which a soul enters into the Sanctuary of Grace and cleave to the Spirit of Truth, take Holy Sanctuary:

Envision the Spiritual Sun in your heart and remember the Indwelling Christ – the Light presence (Messiah) and Light-power (Shekinah of Messiah) within you; then envision a ray of light shooting forth from the Spiritual Sun in your heart, magically appearing in the space before you as the image of the Yeshua Messiah in the Palace of Lights – but rather than facing the Holy Master in the center, with the Master they all face you. (In this visualization the image of St. Lazarus appears next to John the Baptist, and the four archangels appear at the four corners of the envisioned assembly in the space before you; the Woman of Light is above and behind the image of the Holy Master in the center – the emanation of the Holy Womb of Mother Sophia, and the canopy of rainbow glory and pillars supporting it are not visualized.)

This image appears at the level of your brow, and below this image envision a vast field of all manner of sentient beings – including those who are on the path, those not yet on the path and those that oppose the path to enlightenment and all who are on it.

Remember the Holy Mother, Our Lord and Our Lady and the Divine Grace of the Gnostic Revelation embodied in them, and opening your mind, heart and life to them, offer yourself up as a holy vessel of their blessings and grace, and pray for the outpouring of their blessing and grace upon all beings – letting love and compassion for all beings dawn in your heart. Then take up the chant: Yeshua Messiah, Kallah Messiah, Io Adonai, remembering Yeshua Messiah as the Great Gnostic Revealer, the Holy Bride as the Assembly of the Faithful and Elect, and Io Adonai as the Holy Gospel flowing forth from their Mystical Union, with conscious intention to abide in the Holy Sanctuary of Grace.

As you chant, envision the luminous assembly shining upon you and all sentient beings gathered with you, blessing you and all beings with streams of light from their light-bodies – you and all beings shining with supernal glory. Then envision that the entire assembly of sentient beings gathered with you dissolves into fluid flowing light and that they pour into your heart – you as all beings entering into Holy Sanctuary and you becoming as a holy sanctuary to all beings in the Blessed Name.

Then take up the chant: Ah Da Na Yah, Yo Ho Sho Vo Ho, Ma Sa Yah. As you intone this chant, envision the great luminous assembly dissolve into fluid flowing light and pour into the heart center of the Master, the Risen Christ; and envision the Risen Christ dissolve into a light-seed of white brilliance, which shoots to a point above your head, and then passes down through the top of your head and descends through the central channel-way, melting into the Spiritual Sun in your heart. In this way receive the blessing and empowerment of the Holy Master, and be received into the Sanctuary of Grace, the Mystical Body of the Risen Christ. This is the union of Taking Sanctuary and the Generation of the Sacred Heart as a single practice.

Concluding this practice of Taking Sanctuary, give praise and thanksgiving to El Elyon, the True Light, and seal the practice with a Kabbalistic Cross, with the conscious intention of the dedication of blessings to all beings.

Arising in the Threefold Body of Messiah Melchizedek:
Having received the blessing and empowerment of Taking
Sanctuary, abide in Meditation, and remember the Ain Nature of
All as the Body of Truth – the Body of Clear Light Joy, which is
the Body of the Virgin Mother, the Body of the Human One of
Light and Our Beloved Sophia.

Aware of this Holy Body as real only in the experience of the
enlightened ones of the Divine Order, let the holy desire to arise in
the Body of Glory dawn – with that holy desire envision
that you spontaneously arise as a Spiritual Sun in the midst
of infinite space, with rays of light going out into all subtle
dimensions of the realms, worlds and universes of the Entirety.
Aware of how few can receive the Gnostic and Light
Transmission in this way – only those beings of subtle and
sublime existence, or those who are most open and sensitive,
generate the holy desire to assume a Body of Emanation that
may become visible and tangible to them, and envision that you
spontaneously arise as the Divine Image of Risen Savior.
Aware of your abiding in the Sanctuary of Divine Grace, allow
the awareness to dawn of yourself in present incarnation as a
member of the Mystical Body of the Risen Christ – an emanation
of the Human One of Light in this world of the Entirety, all
through the Grace of the Risen Savior.

Intone Hallelu Yah three times, and then intone Amen; abiding in
this conviction.

Walk as a Light-bearer, Healer and Peacemaker – walk in beauty
and holiness. This is the holy seal of this practice – the *Life
Divine*.

Union with the Holy Tzaddik:

Begin with Meditation
Then, envision that your Root Tzaddik magically appears in the
space before you as the Tzaddik of the Messiah, John the Baptist –
his body is as though radiant with sunlight and there is holy fire
in his hair; his camel's hair garment is like white brilliance and his
leather belt great glory, and he bears a holy staff of divine power
in his hand with the Great Name engraved upon it – holy letters
formed of fiery light.

To his left is Our Lord and to his right is Our Lady, behind and
just above him are Enoch and Moses; the Twelve and their
Shekinah Consorts encircle him, and then the greater and lesser
prophets, and then a great assembly of tzaddikim and maggidim,
countless in number – he is Baal Shem, the Master of the Name,
the Archon of the Womb, Great Maggid, Holy Tzaddik.
With adoration of the True Light, the Supernal Light, take up
the chant of the Divine Name, El Elyon; as you chant, envision
the Holy Tzaddik raise his staff and envision lightening bolts of
blessing and grace going out into all directions of limitless
space – purifying limitless space from all shades and shadows,
sanctifying all beings in the name of God Most High.
Then take of the chant of Eheieh-I Am: Ah Ha Yah Ha, and
envision the Holy Tzaddik raising his staff and a bolt of fiery light
descending upon you, entering through the top of your head
and passing down to your feet – your entire subtle body
transformed into this Holy Supernal Light in an instant, all
obstructions dispelled and the fullness of Divine Grace manifest.
Taking up the chant: Yah Ha Sha Va Ha, envision the luminous
assembly dissolve into the Holy Tzaddik; then shifting to the
chant: Ma Sa Yah, envision the Holy Tzaddik dissolve into fluid
flowing light and shooting directly into your heart.

With the chant of Adonai seal this Union, and with the cessation of the chant abide in union as long as you can – aware of the inseparability of the Outer Tzaddik (Root Tzaddik) and Inner Tzaddik, one Holy Tzaddik, within yet ever beyond, Messiah Melchizedek.

This practice is concluded by praise and thanksgiving to El Elyon for the emanations of the Divine Order and manifestation of the Light Transmission lineages, and with prayers for the Light Transmission lineages to remain manifest in the world until the fruition of the harvest of souls; then, the dedication of merit and blessings upon all beings.

*This is the inner Union with the Holy Tzaddik; if the secret Union with the Holy Tzaddik is known it may be performed in place of this practice and is considered most auspicious in blessing power.

Purification of Space:

Taking up the continuum of Union with the Holy Master if there is a need to purify space, from the Spiritual Sun in the center of the head, self-generate as the Risen Christ and from your heart center as the Risen Christ generate your Shekinah Consort as a great aura of fiery light. Then envision this light shoots out in all directions, like waves from a great sphere, dispelling all shades and shadows in an instant. In your mind say, "Amen." In this way space is purified of all negativity, as are all beings in that sacred space.

Extending Peace:

Whenever you enter into a place remember the Spiritual Sun in your heart and remember yourself as an emanation of the Mystical Body of the Risen Christ. Filled with Divine Light, enter as the Human One of Light, an inwardly say, "Peace be upon this place," inwardly intoning: Sha-Lom once. If the peace of the Messiah cannot rest upon the place, let it run and return to you, all as the dance of the Shekinah of Messiah.

The Blessing Way:

In Union with the Holy Master you are the emanation of the Risen Christ and you serve the Christ in all beings – you walk in the Blessing Way. In every possible way you can conceive, visible and invisible, extend blessings to all beings and seek their empowerment. In this way Union with the Holy Master is actualized and realized – embodied; no longer are you the doer, but rather the Risen Christ and Holy Spirit is the doer, all is accomplished by Divine Grace.

*In this continuum of practice it is good to perform the Wedding Feast at least once a week.

This is the essential continuum of Union with the Holy Master –

May all who take it up be blessed and empowered to bring it to fruition, and in fruition may all beings be blessed with the peace and joy of the Risen Christ;
amen.

Practice of the Vow with the Great Maggidims

The Sacred Rite:

Let the Templar face the East and remember the Human one of Light and our Beloved Sophia, the Continuum of Light Transmission of which they stand as a guardian, and let them call upon the name of El Elyon, the True Light, remembering the mystery of the Order of Melchizedek.

Then let the Templar draw her or his sword, and turning it upright in the position of salutations proclaim:

Kodesh, kodesh, kodesh Yahweh Elohim Tzavaot – Holy, holy, holy is the LORD God of Hosts

Baruch Ha-Shem – Blessed is the Name of the LORD, now and forever. Amen.

Let the Templar turn and face the South, calling upon Ha-Shem and invoking the Great Maggid, saying:

In the Blessed Name of Adonai, I call upon you, Michael, One-Like-Unto-God, Come, Archangel, as Commander of the Hosts of the Light Realm, And bear witness to the speaking of my Holy Vow – Come with your hosts, and let us manifest Holy Sanctuary for the faithful and elect!

Then let the Templar take up the traditional chant of Archangel Michael:

Ya Ha Va Ha Ma Mi Ha El
As the Templar takes up the chant, let them envision Archangel Michael magically appearing in the space before them, along with his celestial host who number as the stars in the Milky Way.

The visualization:

Michael appears clad in warrior's garb, bearing a sword of
flashing fire, like that of the Great Kerub, and his sword is drawn.
He assumes a human form with two great wings, and his head
is as though hollow, filled with sunlight, so that brilliant light
shoots forth form his eyes, nose and mouth. His is a vast presence
and there is a great and glorious light about him. He comes
with his angelic hosts, countless in number, and they form a
sacred circle around you – it is as though you stand in infinite
space in the midst of the Milky Way, but rather than among the
stars, you stand in the midst of a great company of holy angels.
It is a beautiful and awesome vision, the entire image being
formed of the most subtle translucent light, yet shining with a
immeasurable brilliance.

Having invoked the Great Maggid and the host of maggidim,
holding the envisioned image in mind, in the presence of the
Great Maggid, let the Templar remember the Divine Order of
Tzaddikim and Maggidim, and let them remember the Way
of the Righteous Warrior – let them speak their Vow in Holy
Remembrance.

Then let the Templar pray for the manifestation of the Holy
Sanctuary and guardianship of the Continuum of Light
Transmission on earth, and let them pray for the shattering of the
dominion of the klippot, liberation from the domination of the
demiurge, and the driving out of the darkness from the people
and the land – all in remembrance of the Risen Messiah and
Shekinah of Messiah, the Lord and Holy Bride.

Let the Templar turn to face the West and let them turn the
sword to point down towards the earth, let them pray for the
fruition of the Divine Revelation and Peace on Earth – the fruition
of Supernal or Messianic Consciousness in humanity, and let
them give honor to those who have sojourned in the Grail Quest
before them, those who have labored before them for the Second
Coming, the *Reception of the Holy Bride*.

Then let the Templar turn and face the North, and let them sheath the sword and pray for the embodiment of the Truth and Light, and the extension of the True Light in the world – all in the remembrance of the countless world-systems through which the Light Transmission has passed before entering into this Good Earth.

At the conclusion of this prayer, let the Templar intone AGLA; and as they turn to face the East once again let them intone Atoh Givor Leolam Adonai; then, facing East, let them proclaim: You are heroic for the world, O Lord!

Then let the Templar lay down the sword and let them pray for the people, and let them give praise and thanks to El Elyon, the Divine Most High, and giving glory to the Name of the LORD. In closing, let them speak the Holy Seal, offering the glory of the practice to El Elyon and dedicating the merit generated to the people – to all sentient beings.

This concludes the practice of speaking the Holy Vow before the Great Maggid.

*Occasionally, a Wedding Feast (or Holy Eucharist) may be included as part of this ceremonial practice; typically as an extension of the practice at the end.

In essence, this is a method for clearing a space of negative forces and manifesting sacred space. Thus, Templar initiates will often modify this practice, removing the speaking of the vow when helping to manifest sacred space in service to the Continuum and Priesthood (the Sanctuary of Bet El); but when manifesting sacred space for their own theurgic work the speaking of the vow remains in place.

*On a Templar altar there is often the Sword and Grail, three candles (white, red and black), a cross, a container of holy water and vial of holy oil, and there may also be images of the Master of the Order (Yeshua Messiah) and Our Lady (or else the Virgin Mother). Other altar arrangements are also used for the sake of

theurgic workings, but this is the most common
version of the Templar altar. (The Templar altar is usually in the
East of the Sanctuary, though not always.)

May we stand as righteous warriors, peacemakers, honoring our
vow; amen.

Sacred vow of the Order of the Knights Templars .

The Vow is as follows:
Do not fear in the face of the Enemy;
Do not lie, but live by the Spirit of Truth, even on the pain of death;
Love the Holy One,
with all your heart and soul,
mind and strength; Love Wisdom;
Defend the orphan and widow,
the poor, the outcast and the oppressed; Cultivate love and compassion,
and stand as a righteous warrior;
Guard the Holy Grail,
and the Order of the Grail; Bring peace;
Do not do what you hate.

This vow becomes the spiritual practice of the knight or dame of the Order of the Knights Templars and has outer, inner and secret levels of interpretation and meaning, which are drawn out through prayer, contemplation and meditation on the vow, as well as listening and hearing oral teachings associated with the vow.

One practice given to new chevaliers for contemplation of the vow is as follows:

With sword drawn and upraised, invoke the Great Maggid and speak your vow before the Holy Shekinah of Messiah; and pray to receive the knowledge, understanding and wisdom of the vow, and empowerment to uphold it.

When you sheath your sword, remember peace and pray for peace in the world, and pray to be empowered as a peacekeeper. (If you are willing, remember your duty and offer your life each day to the service of the Divine Will and Divine Sovereignty.)

In this way remember your vow so that you might live by it.
Amen.

Through this practice, quite naturally, new knights and dames
become intimately acquainted with the Vow of the Order; yet, as
simple as it may seem on the surface, it is also a powerful theurgic
gesture in this practice, which is played upon and drawn out
by other practices that are given to the knight or dame as they
progress in the service of the Order.

Holy Vow (for the use in group)

O Knights and Dames of the Holy Grail,
O Initiates of the Order of Knights Templar,
Let us draw the sword and give salutations,
And let us remember our vow before the Master, When he spoke,
saying –
Do not fear in the face of the Enemy;
Do not lie, but live by the Spirit of Truth, even on the pain of
death;
Love the Holy One,
with all your heart and soul,
mind and strength; Love Wisdom;
Defend the orphan and widow,
the poor, the outcast and the oppressed; Cultivate love and
compassion,
and stand as a righteous warrior;
Guard the Holy Grail,
and the Order of the Grail; Bring peace;
Do not do what you hate.
This is our vow,
We remember it,
And we shall honor it, Before the Master,
We speak it, Before the sword, We swear it; Amen.

+

This is a traditional opening invocation from rites within the
Order of Knights Templars, when Templars of the Order gather
together for a celebration of the mysteries of the Order and for
theurgic workings. At times, however, it is modified and used as
a practice of speaking the vow by individual Templars in their
morning session. When used as a spiritual practice apart from an
assembly, the Templar remembers their sisters and brothers who
stand in circle with them, as well as the sisters and brothers of the
Order at large, and envisions the entire assembly of the Order
all gathered in the inner dimension of the sacred space; likewise,
they envision the "celestial Templars" among the assembly, the
angelic hosts of Archangel Michael who are
as the "holy guardian angels" or angelic forms of the sisters
and brothers gathered together. In this practice of speaking the

vow the initiate is facing the east throughout the practice, and envisions the Master of the Order, the Risen Messiah. in the east as the holy vow is spoken – the luminous assembly represents the Shekinah of Messiah, the Holy Bride, and the Risen Messiah is the image of the Spiritual Sun that shines in the heart of every member of the Mystical Body.

After the opening proclamation, before speaking the vow, the sword is unsheathed and uplifted so that it is before initiate's face, and as the Templar speaks the vow their head is slightly bowed in honor of the Perfect Master. As the third section of the vow is spoken, the sword is turned down, tip of the sword upon the ground, and the Templar kneels on one knee, envisioning the image of Our Lady emanating from the heart center of the Master with a holy sword in her hand, performing the rite of dubbing as when the Templar received their initiation into the Order. Rising to their feet, the Templar sheaths their sword, praying for the extension of Divine Light and Peace in the world, and envisions the entire luminous display dissolving into fluid flowing light, and pouring into their heart center – the Spiritual Sun shining brightly within them.

When performed in circle, in an actual assembly of Templars, all stand in a circle facing inward, and the Holy Master is envisioned in the center of the circle; if a sacred tau of the Divine Order is present, she or he may take a position in the center of the circle, or they may take up a position in the center of the east, depending on the nature of the ceremony being performed in the gathering.

The invocation of St. Michael is not performed during the speaking of the vow because, typically the invocation of St. Michael follows immediately after the speaking of the vow in theurgic movement of the assembly; thus it is not included in this practice of speaking the holy vow.

If this us used by a Templar as an individual practice, frequently, following the completion of the practice the sword will be laid either upon the altar or in front of the altar on the ground, and turning to the west, he or she will envision Archangel Michael magically emanating from their body of light. Then the Templar will intone:

Kodesh, kodesh, kodesh Yahweh Elohim Tzavaot – Holy, holy, holy is the LORD God of Hosts!

Following this, they will take up the traditional chant of Archangel Michael (Ya Mi Ha Michael, or Ya Ha Va Ha Ma Mi Ha El), with the conscious intention of the guardianship of the sacred circle and continuum of light transmission on earth, the guardianship of human evolution to Christ Consciousness. (This includes the intention of the evolution of all sentient beings to Christ Consciousness, for all are in the Human One of Light.) At the conclusion of the chant the Templar will envision union with Archangel Michael, drawing the divine emanation once again into their body of light, and abiding in the awareness of the Divine I Am, the Templar will proclaim:

Be gone, O evil spirits!
Behold, the dominion of the klippot is shattered and the holy sparks are gathered into the Mystical Body of the Risen Christ; all darkness is driven out from the people and the land, all are drawn up in the Great Ascension, the remembrance of the Light Realm!

As it has been spoken; so is it done: amen.

When the Templar speaks this proclamation, they envision an explosion of light from their heart center, akin to a blast of a spiritual nuclear fire going into all directions of endless space, envisioning all manifest in the Pleroma of Light – as though all becomes Divine and Supernal Light in an instant.

Then the Templar speaks the Holy Seal upon the practice, praying for blessings and grace to go out to all beings, and dedicating the merit of their practice to the glory of El Elyon and the benefit of all beings. This concludes the invocation of St. Michael in this version of speaking the holy vow.

Once this practice is accomplished the Templar may proceed to other spiritual practice or may go on to other theurgic work to be done.

The purpose of practices of speaking the vow, aside from their theurgic intention, is to empower the Templar to walk as a spiritual or righteous warrior, remembering their vow in their daily lives. Thus going out into the world following the practice of speaking the vow, the Templar seeks to embody this vow in their thoughts, speech and actions: *this is the practice of realization*.

May we be empowered to walk in the world as One-Like-Unto-God; amen.

Secrets of the Risen Christ

There is an essential practice in our lineage, which is not ascribed to any specific order, but which is used by initiates of all orders – the "Yeshua Brow Practice." This is the basis of the Light Mind Palace of the Risen Christ in the Order of Knights Templars; thus it is a preliminary to the generation of this Palace of Lights. The practice is as follows. Yeshua Brow Practice:

Abiding in Meditation, set your attention on your brow, and with conscious intention intone the Blessed Name of Yeshua Messiah into the center of your head; as a practice among Templars of the Order the chant Yah Ha Sha Va Ha Ma Sa Yah can be used, joining the practice to their continuum of Union with the Holy Master. The practice is nothing more of less than this, and there is no visualization, but all that arises occurs naturally and spontaneously without being conjured.

Of this practice it is said, "It opens one's sight to the World of the Holy Spirit – the Light Realm."

If one is blessed to encounter a tzaddik or apostle of the tradition and the necessary conditions are in place, the full force of this practice is founded upon an empowerment that can be transmitted; nevertheless, however, taking up the practice apart from the empowerment can prove very effective, for by practicing it some have received empowerment on subtle levels or through a movement of the Grace of the Risen Savior.

*This practice is typically a preliminary practice of the Risen Christ, as the natural and spontaneous arising of the "Light Mind" (Mochin Or) is the perfect empowerment for this Palace of Lights, in which case the practice of this Holy Palace can serve as the integration of the Light Mind with the mind, heart and life of the initiate.

If an initiate is seeking to shift from the practice of Putting on the Name of the Lord to the practice of the Light Mind Palace, along with a natural arising of the experience of Light Mind, a continuum of prayer and meditation seeking the movement of the Holy Spirit should be taken up; either that or seeking a special blessing or an empowerment from one's Holy Tzaddik – for the timing of beginning such practices is not on a whim, but rather initiates seek to discern auspicious circumstances that might remove unnecessary obstructions. Such spiritual practices are generated from the realization of adepts and masters in the lineage, and are holy, and we approach them in a sacred manner with mindfulness and reverence. (How we approach such thing determines what they are to us, and likewise will determine their power and effectiveness.)

Here it must be said that the tendency to practice this and that in a casual fashion is a sever obstruction to full generation and fruition of the continuum of practice – such practices do not bear good fruit by a single application, several applications, or fitful and inconsistent application, but rather they bear good fruit over time, when consistently applied for a prolonged duration, with proper development. This is true of most spiritual practices – the ideal is a *continuum of practice* that may serve as a vehicle for the unfolding of the Light Transmission and Self-realization in Christ.

Along with this it must be said that it is important that an initiate does not confuse recognition or peak experience with realization – the "vision of experience" must become "pure vision," which is to say recognition must be integrated into the mind, heart and body to become actual Self-realization. Experiencing something of the Truth and Light, we must then labor in the spiritual life and practice to live according to it – to actualize and realize it, and to embody it: this, alone, is *actual realization*.

Light Mind Palace:
Abide in Meditation and envision the arising of the clear crystal light-body.

Then take up the chant of Eheieh-I Am: Ah Ha Yah, and envision a sphere of brilliant white diamond-like light magically appear in the center of your head; along with this center, also envision a straight channel-way appear from this center of white brilliance to your root star (center), and envision the root, navel, solar plexus and heart stars magically appear – green, golden, blue and red, respectively; but as relatively small dim lights at the outset. (These colors of the centers are distinctly different that the typical attributes when working with seven centers.)

Focusing on the holy star of white brilliance in the center of your head and gathering your consciousness into it, take up the chant: Yah Ha Sha Va Ha, and envision this sphere expanding, doubling its size, and growing brighter and brighter, and envision rays of jeweled light going out in four directions – golden/east, blue/west, red/south and green/north, the "east" being in front of you. These rays magically appear as four brilliant light seeds of the corresponding colors, and as they appear an inverse pyramid of diamond-like light magically appears around your body – apex at your feet and base at your brow, the light seeds at the four corners of a diamond square if looked at from above. (As you envision this, remember, with your consciousness gathered into the sphere of white brilliance in your head, you arise *as this holy star*; likewise, with the plane of the pyramid's base at the brow, it is as though the top of the head is open to infinite space above – there, in the midst, you shine radiant as the holy star, with four emanated lights surrounding you.)

When the essential lights are generated by the sound-vibration of this holy chant, then take up the chant: Yo Ho Vo Sho Ho, and envision these light seed magically transforming into the holy letters of the Blessed Name, each light seed according to its proper correspondence as known from the practice Putting on the Name of the Lord, with you as the sphere of white brilliance arising as the Holy Shin in the center.

Then, taking up the two chants together: Yah Ha Sha Va Ha, Yo Ho Vo Sho Ho; envision yourself magically self-generating as the image of the Risen Christ in the center, and envision the four jeweled letters magically transforming into the Four Archangels of the Palace – Raphael/East, Gavriel/West, Michael/South and Uriel/North, and with the arising of these images envision the entire Palace of Lights appearing as your self-emanation.

You arise in the center as the Risen Christ, with four emanated archangels surrounding you – your body is as though composed of sunlight, your robes as though of violet light, with an inner robe of white brilliance, and there is a great rainbow aura surrounding you; you are enthroned on a red rose throne of seventy-two petals, the wisdom of the Baal Shem, Master of the Name. (You are holding the Vase of Wisdom and the Scepter of the Living Word.)

The four archangels stand before jeweled gates (at the corners of the palace) corresponding in color to their emanation bodies, and they have human bodies with the faces of the corresponding Kerubim, and four great wings – Raphael the face of the Human One, Gavriel the face of the Eagle, Michael the face of the Lion and Uriel the face of the Ox. The outer robe of each is the corresponding color of its dominion and their inner robes are white brilliance, and each is wearing a corresponding jeweled diamond pendant set in gold – golden topaz, sapphire, ruby and emerald colored diamonds, but celestial stones such as are not found upon the earth. Raphael bears a holy sword and a scroll, Gavriel bears a holy grail and a scroll, Michael bears a holy staff (with the great name engraved on it) and a scroll, and Uriel bears a holy pentacle (with heavenly bread on it) and a scroll – all stand before their gates facing inward.

You are in the center of the Palace and there are Four Living Pillars surrounding you, aligned with the "cross-quarters," like a square turned at a forty five degree angle to the greater square of the Palace – these are formed of jeweled light and support a great rainbow canopy of translucent light above, beyond which is the image of the Woman of Light, as in the Apocalypse, straight above your head as the Emanation Body of the Risen Christ. Beneath the canopy, to your left and right, hovers Enoch and Elijah, and enthrone to your left and to your right on white rose thrones are the Holy Mother (blue robes) and Holy Bride (red robes) respectively, before you is John the Baptist and behind you is St. Lazarus, then there is a circle of the twelve saviors with shekinah consorts (twelve holy apostles) and twenty-four male and female elders surrounding them, and then the circle of greater and lesser prophets, and the patriarchs and matriarchs, and then circles upon circles of holy tzaddikim and maggidim, countless in number. (As the center of the Holy Palace, the emanation of the Risen Christ, all face you.)

The ground of this Palace of Light is like a vast firmament of clear diamond-like light sparkling with brilliant rainbows hues that move in spiral patterns throughout the Palace, and it is the manifestation of the Great Ofan below; the ceiling is an infinite expands of spacious clear light, like a predawn sky, though unimaginably self-radiant, and it is the manifestation of the Great Ofan above. This Great Palace fills infinite space, and is infinitely large and infinitely small at one and the same time – it is a Pure Light Realm, all the emanation of your emanated Glory Body as the Risen Christ, the Human One of Light.

All of this emanates from your Body of Glory as the holy chant is intoned, as though streams of light and glory spontaneously flow out of your Great Light-Body and magically appear as the various aspects of this body of vision – all formed of the most subtle, yet brilliant, translucent light, like a vast rainbow in the primordial ground of Clear Light.

When the Holy Palace is emanated from you as the Risen Christ, with the great luminous assembly gathered around you, take up the chant: Ah Ha Yah, Yah Ha Va Ha, Sha Da Da Yah, Ah Da Na Yah – Sho (prolonging the "O" as a long vowel). As you chant, envision yourself as the Risen Christ and the entire Palace of your Emanation Body growing more and more brilliant, and envision the Supernal Light passing down from your Glory Body as the Risen Christ into the crystalline light body below, awakening the four lower interior stars along the central channel-way of clear light – your Light Mind as the Risen Christ (Supramental Light) passing down into the emanated light-body of incarnation, then ascending again into your Glory Body as the Risen Christ above.

Then, as the Risen Christ, along with your emanated luminous assembly, intone: Ah Yah Da Ha Na Va Yah Ha – Sha (prolonging the "A" as a short vowel). As you chant, envision an influx of white brilliance passing down through the central channel-way of clear light and envision the dissolution of the centers into one another from root to heart and into the brow – you emanated as the Risen Christ, receiving the ascent in your heart center as the Risen Savior.

As the Risen Christ, contemplate the bondage of sentient beings throughout the Entirety, and the immeasurable sorrow and suffering of their experience dwelling in ignorance of the Pleroma of Light – and in the Light Mind allow the awareness of the countless realms, worlds and universes of the Entirety to arise, and the great need for the emanations of the Holy Savior, the Human One of Light. Then with conscious intention of countless emanations of yourself going out into all realms, worlds and universes of the Entirety, with your emanated great luminous assembly take up the chant: Yah Ah Ha Da Va Na Ha Yah, sending out emanations of yourself for the sake of the enlightenment and liberation of all beings – envisioning emanations going into various realms, worlds and universe. (This grand vision must arise naturally and spontaneously in a supramental state, as it cannot be described in terms of ordinary mental consciousness. Thus, unless it spontaneously arises do not worry about the visualization, but the focus is the Palace of Lights and the conscious intention of countless emanations going into all dominions of the entirety, and this is enough to accomplish it.) Then, as the Risen Christ with great luminous assembly, take up the dissolution and ascension chant once again: Ah Yah Da Ha Na Va Yah Ha, with the conscious intention of running and returning from the realms, worlds and universes of the Entirety, the dissolution of all realms, worlds and universes of the Entirety, and the drawing up of all sentient beings in the Great Resurrection and Ascension with you – gathering the All into your Sacred Heart. (Again, if there is a vision of this it will arise naturally and spontaneously; but regardless, it is accomplished purely with the conscious intention.)

Now with great luminous assembly, take up the chant: Yah Ah Ha Ha Va Yah Ha Ha, and envision the entire Palace all at once dissolving into fluid flowing light and pouring into your Sacred Heart as the Risen Christ – knowing this as the fruition of your Holy Desire to liberate all beings; and envision your Glory Body as the Risen Christ dissolving and condensing to become like a Holy Star in the "head" that is now No Head – then intoning "Ah" three times dissolve into the Clear Light Ground, like a rainbow disappearing in the sky!

When the mind-stream moves from this repose, envision yourself, as yourself, spontaneously arising in a jeweled light-body, all five centers fully opened and set in their place; then intone Ah Ha Yah Ha Va Ha – Yo Ho Vo Sho Ho, and envision the diamond-like light of white brilliance from your brow star filling your whole body – you an emanation of the Human One of Light in the world.

Abiding in this Holy Awareness of Pure Emanation, with conscious intention of all beings receiving the blessing and grace of the One Anointed with the Supernal Light of El Elyon, take up the chant: Yah Ha Sha Va Ha Ma Sa Yah, envisioning the extension of Divine Light from your Body of Light going out to all the world and all who dwell in it – this the Light of the True Cross (Shin Tau, the Great Seth).

When you complete the chant cycle, abide in this awareness as long as you can.

Then, in fruition of the cycle of practice, give praise and thanksgiving to the El Elyon (the Divine Most High), and to all of the tzaddikim and maggidim of the Divine Order (Order of Melchizedek), and prayer for the continued manifestation of the Continuum of Light Transmission in this world until all is accomplished; then dedicate the energy-intelligence generated by your practice to all beings. This concludes the practice of the Light Mind Palace of the Risen Christ.

This practice may be modified to accomplish all manner of works of invisible assistance, for all wonderworking power of the theurgic art is in it – it is an advanced practice that is very effective when the Templar has prepared the ground of their consciousness appropriately. Many initiates have experienced the dawn of non-dual realization through this holy meditation.
*In the case of initiates trained in traditional circles, who have received instruction in the Four Base Rituals – at times, through cycles of practice using the Four Base Rituals, this Union can be integrated to an active theurgic continuum to extend invisible assistance. Essentially, the continuum of Union with the Holy Master serves as the generation of Divine or Enlightened Energy, which is then directed through a theurgic continuum that extends divine assistance to specific individuals known to the initiate. However, proper training and development of the Four Base Rituals requires actual involvement in a circle for a prolonged period of time, as there is no way to communicate exactly how the sacred rituals are performed in writing – any writings of the rituals can only serve as a support to an experiential and oral transmission.

May the writing and publishing of this holy practice be a blessings upon all beings; may it invoke Divine Light into the world; and may it serve to facilitate the liberation of those who take it up with a good heart; amen.

The Sword of the Templar

St. Paul instructs us, saying:

"Finally, be strong in Adonai an in the strength of his power. Put on the whole armor of god, so that you may stand against the wiles of the devil. For our struggle is not against enemies of blood and flesh, but against the archons, against authorities, against the cosmic powers of this present darkness, against spiritual forces of evil in heavenly places. Therefore take up the whole armor of God, so that you may be able to withstand on that evil day, and having done everything, to stand firm. Stand therefore, and fasten the belt of truth around your waist, and put on the breastplate of righteousness. As shoes for your feet put on whatever will make you ready to proclaim the Gospel of Peace (Shalom). With all of these, take the shield of faith, with which you will be able to quench all of the flaming arrows of the evil one. Take the helmet of salvation, and the sword of the Spirit, which is the word of God. Pray in the Spirit at all times in every prayer and supplication. To that end keep alert and always persevere in supplication for all of the saints" (Ephesians 6:10-18).

This passage from the New Testament is a central contemplation and meditation of Templar initiates, for having been dubbed a Knight of the Holy Temple in the Order of the Knights Templars the initiate puts on the Blessed Name and the whole armor of God, just as St. Paul instructs us – this is the "Charge of the Templar," and a Reciting of the Charge often accompanies the Speaking of the Vow. Quite naturally, as there are many teachings in our Holy Order regarding the Holy Vow, so there are many teachings regarding this passage of scripture, all as instruction in the Way of the Templar, the Way of the Spiritual Warrior, the Exorcist.

Here we may explore some of the teachings given on this passage for the sake of our knowledge and understanding, praying that the Holy Spirit illuminates us as to the deeper and more esoteric meaning, and praying for the guardianship of the faithful and elect from the incursions of archonic and demonic forces.

When St. Paul speaks of the spiritual forces of wickedness or evil he is speaking of cosmic and spiritual forces bound up in cosmic ignorance – the dominion of the demiurge, the dominion of the klippot; hence, he is speaking of the illusion of separation that pervades the Realm of Perud, the Entirety. These spiritual forces of ignorance or darkness have no root in Atzilut, the Pleroma of Light, but through the process of tzimtzum (restriction) in creation they come into being in Beriyah, and hold dominion in Yetzirah and Asiyah.

At the level of Beriyah these are great cosmic divinities that stand with unimaginable power like that of the holy archangels of God, but in complete ignorance of the source of their divine power, God, the True Light; at the level of Yetzirah are their hosts, which are composed lesser divinities and all manner of spiritual beings-forces bearing power akin to the holy angels of God, but abiding in ignorance of the True God, El Elyon. The power of this dominion of the demiurge and archons – the dominion of the klippot, extends into Asiyah as the spirits of the celestial spheres, the stars, sun, moon and planets, as opposed to their divine intelligences; hence, the klippot of the Sphere of Mazlot, or Sphere of Heimarmene, the Sphere of Fate (law of karma).
*As well as the celestial influences, these spiritual forces are also expressed through the impure elements.

Thus, truly, as St. Paul teaches us, these spiritual forces of klippot are established in "heavenly places" and celestial spheres, having their root in Beriyah among the great cosmic powers.

The demiurge, cosmic ignorance, the illusion of separation, comes into being at the level of Da'at in Beriyah, and the power of the ignorance increases in Yetzirah and Asiyah exponentially as the Divine Light becomes more and more restricted – at the level of Malkut of Malkut in Asiyah, which corresponds to the material dimension of the world, the dominion of the klippot is almost complete; thus, on account of a virtual complete ignorance, a grand illusion of separation, in this "present ignorance" archonic and demonic forces rule the world.

Essentially, in ignorance, souls have little or no discernment of spiritual forces, and bound up in ego-grasping, and egoistic desire and fear, completely self-identified with name and form, and personal history, bound up in the desire to receive for self alone (the evil inclination), and having desire only for the world and things of the world, souls are dominated by the influence of klippotic forces, and becoming dominated by these archonic and demonic forces, they become vehicles of the dominion of those spiritual forces in the world. Indeed, as we witness with the plight of fundamental and orthodox religions in the world, these spiritual forces of wickedness even come to stand in the place of God, the True Light, so that believing that they worship and serve the True Light, many among the faithful worship and serve the dominion of the demiurge and archons, being deceived by the false lights of the klippot.

Thus, truly, as St. Paul teaches us, our "struggle is not against enemies of blood and flesh" but is against the power of the demiurge and archons, the dominion of the klippot; as the Lord prayed upon the cross for the people, so shall we pray: "Father, forgive them, for they do not know what they are doing." Here we must say, the dominion of the klippot, the dominion of the demiurge and archons, depends upon our egotism and selfish ambitions – the root of all evil lies in ego-grasping, and egoistic desire and fear, the evil inclination, which is the desire to receive for self alone; rooting ego-grasping out of yourself, and bringing the evil inclination into the service of the good inclination, transforming it, is the Way of the Great Exodus and is call the "complete exorcism of all evil," and it is the power that corresponds to the sword of the Templar, the Sword of Truth. Looking and seeing, and coming to understand the great conflict of cosmic and spiritual forces within and behind all that transpires in this world, and within and behind what transpires in all realms, worlds and universes of the Entirety, we know and understand the need for salvation, the need for the Sanctuary of Grace manifest by our Lord and Savior, the Gnostic Revealer; for apart from the Sanctuary of Grace, the power of the Blessed Name of Yeshua, no soul would pass up in the ascent of the

Great Exodus or escape the dominion of the demiurge – no soul would be enlightened and liberated. Thus, looking and seeing, and coming to understand this great conflict of forces, the zeal of our faith will wax strong and hot, and we will be empowered to a passionate cleaving to the Messiah and Shekinah of Messiah. Indeed, in this we will know and understand our need for the Savior, Yeshua Messiah, and the Holy Grail that heals all wounds and gives eternal youth, eternal life, and we will know our need to put on the Blessed Name and the full armor of God, cleaving to the Spiritual Sun of El Elyon.

Here it must be said, that those in modern times within "liberal churches" who claim to have faith in Yeshua Messiah as Lord and Savior, and claim to have faith in the Holy Gospel, but who then say that they do not believe in dark and hostile forces, proposing that they are an "archaic idea," as though "outdated," do not have the fullness of true faith and the gnosis of Christ, for as yet they do not know and understand the need for the Sanctuary of Grace and do not have the cause in place to passionately cleave and to rejoice in the Risen Messiah. Truly, such suggestions are a breech of faith that reflects the greater deception in these dark and perverse times. Essentially, such disbelief serves the interests of archonic and demonic influences, for when people no longer believe in the influences of cosmic and spiritual forces of evil they no longer know to resist and banish them – shades and shadows are free to their play in the human heart and mind, and run riot! Now, if we want to know and understand the power of the Blessed Name and the armor of God, and we want to know and understand the Sanctuary of Grace established in the Risen Messiah, we may consider the story of the namesake of our Holy Order that is told by St. John in Revelation – the story of St. Michael set into action by the Holy Child of the Virgin of Light in chapter twelve of the Book of Apocalypse:

"And a war broke out in heaven; Michael and his angels fought against the dragon. The dragon and his angels fought back, but they were defeated, and there was no longer any place for them in heaven.

126

The great dragon was thrown down, that ancient serpent, who is called the Devil and Satan, the deceiver of the whole world – he was thrown down to earth, and his angels were thrown down with him" (Revelation 12:7-9).

This is the power of the Blessed Name of the Risen Messiah in ascension – the opening of the way and leading souls in the Great Exodus, not as Moses, who could only lead the children of Israel out of Egypt to wander aimless in the wilderness, leading from one bondage to another, but leading souls in the Great Liberation from all bondage, uplifting souls from the Entirety into the Pleroma of Light. Through the Holy Cross, as appears on the robes of Templars, in the Blessed Name, the power of the archons and demons is made null and void, and with the power of the full armor of God, as St. Michael and his angels wear, Yaldabaot and his great shadow, Satan, and all of the archons and demons, are made subject and cast out.

Here we must speak a mystery, for having come to the great aeon of St. Michael, before that golden age of the great aeon of St. Rafael dawns, the age of the Holy Spirit and Reception of the Holy Bride, we have come into the Dark Age – as spoken by all true prophets, it is a time of the incarnation of great forces of darkness and chaos, along with great luminous and divine powers; thus, the labor of the spiritual warrior is crucial in these times, the spiritual defense and guardianship of the faithful and elect in the Continuum. This speaks of the holy mystery of the two swords of the Templar initiate, as reflected in a passage from the Gospel of St. Luke. Speaking to his disciples in the upper room just before their departure to the Mount of Olives, Adonai Yeshua says to them:

"When I sent you out without a purse, bag, or sandals, did you lack anything?" They said, "No, not a thing." He said to them, "But now, the one who has a purse must take it, and likewise a bag. And the one who has no sword must sell his cloak and but one. For I tell you, this scripture must be fulfilled in me, 'And he was counted among the lawless': and indeed what was written about me is being fulfilled," They said, "Adonai, look, here are two swords." He replied, "It is enough." (22:35-38)

One holy sword of the Templar is the Knight's sword, the power and dominion of the word of God in the alien realm, the material world, and the other is the magical sword, the power and dominion of the word of God in the spiritual world; hence, one is of the earthly ministry and its defense, and the other is of the heavenly ministry and its guardianship – all as ordained by El Elyon, the Supreme, all in the Way of Melchizedek, the priest-king of righteousness, the priest-king of peace.

Thus, in the Knight's sword is the power to subjugate and destroy evil that appears in the world – to turn the tides of fate and destiny through actions of the life-power, and in the magical sword is the power to cast out the influence of the archonic and demonic forces from the astral earth, elemental realms, celestial spheres and heavens, all in the Blessed Name of the Risen Messiah, all with the power of the full armor of God.

Now we may consider teachings on the armor of God and this Charge of the Knight's Templar, which begins: "Therefore, take up the whole armor of God, so that you may be able to withstand on that evil day, and having done everything, to stand firm." The "evil day" has been explained – it is the Dark Age that has come and is coming, and to stand firm is revealed in the very first line of our Holy Vow, "Do not fear in the face of the Enemy…" According to the holy apostle, St. Paul, the armor of God is to be donned in whole, which is to say, putting on the Blessed Name in full and abiding in the Sanctuary of Grace in full – with all your heart, and with all your soul, and with all your mind and with all your strength, all your life.

This armor of God corresponds to the Holy Sefirot of Atzilut, which is to say it corresponds to the Mystical Body of the Risen Messiah – thus, in reciting this holy charge there are kavvanot, both simple and esoteric; from the simple the esoteric are gleaned. To fasten the belt of truth corresponds to Hod and Netzach – the Divine Name of Yahweh Elohim Tzavaot, the Lord God of Spirits, and it is submission to the dominion of God, the True Light, and to the Living Word of God in you, the Divine Presence and Power of the Messiah that indwells you. In this we shall say, "Gird your loins, and remember and honor the sign of the covenant – sublimate and master the Serpent Power, desire-energy."

To put on the breastplate of righteousness corresponds to Yesod – the Divine Name of Shaddai, the Almighty, and it is right discernment of spiritual forces, severing all links with klippot and cultivating your connection with the Holy Sefirot; hence, to be and become as St. Michael, "One-Who-Is-Like-Unto-God."

These shoes for your feet that prepare and empower you to preach the Gospel of Peace correspond to Hesed and Gevurah – the Divine Names of El and Elohim, and it is selfpurification and self-discipline, coupled with acts of loving-kindness or good works.

To take the shield of faith corresponds with Malkut – the Divine Name Adonai, and it is cleaving to the Holy Shekinah of the Messiah and living according to your faith, which is the definition of righteousness according to the Holy Scriptures.

The helmet of salvation corresponds to Tiferet – the Divine Names of Yahweh and Yeshua Messiah, and it is the Perfect Thunder Intelligence, the Mind of Christ; it is letting Christ and the Holy Spirit take up your person and life, now and always, and in everything.

This brings us to the holy sword of the Spirit, which is the word of God, corresponding to the Supernals – the Divine Names of El Elyon, Eheieh, Yah and Yahweh Elohim, and it is the power of the Divine Light from above, the Supernal Influx, which is the true Divine Power of the Risen Messiah; indeed, this is knowledge and understanding of the Holy Gospel, and it is the empowerment to proclaim the Gospel, pacifying, enriching, subjugating and destroying, all as ordained by El Elyon. (In fruition, this is non-dual realization, Supernal Realization – Messianic Consciousness.)

In this you may know and understand the armor of God so as to put it on, for putting on the Blessed Name, calling upon Ha-Shem and Reciting the Charge, with sword in one hand and the bible in the other, preaching the Gospel of Peace in any space you will enact the pacification, enrichment, subjugation and destruction of all archonic and demonic forces, and you will serve as a defender to the faithful and elect, enacting and guarding the Continuum of Light Transmission.

On the occasion that a greater influx of the Divine Presence and Power is needed, and the Holy Spirit inspires it, to this may be added the invocation of the Archangels and Orders of Angels, along with the celestial intelligences, all as in the Great Convocation, but as the manifestation of the armies of God in guardianship of the Holy Grail and Order of the Grail.

Now the empowerment to all of this is within the daily continuum of prayer, as taught in the
Order – in the case of the Templar initiate, there is a special focus upon defense of the faithful
and elect, and guardianship of the true Gnostic Apostolic Succession and Continuum of Light
Transmission.

Of praying in the Spirit, we can say this: In true prayer, prayer comes from the intelligence of the heart – faith, hope and love, and it is the Holy Spirit that prays with, in and through us; in prayer, as in all things, the spiritual warrior in Christ is no longer the doer of the work, but it is Christ and the Holy Spirit that accomplishes everything, Christ who is victorious in the Templar. This represents the basic oral introduction to this passage from St. Paul's Letter to the Ephesians – if the Spirit is willing, perchance, through study and contemplation of these teachings, and through prayer and meditation, the deeper mysteries will be drawn out; as it is, the keys of deeper meanings as they are understood by adept initiates of our Holy Order have been given in what has been written.

The Templar belt

This is the belt that holds the sword on the side of a Templar – and the keyword of this part of the Armor of God is self-restraint, self-disciple; the evil inclination, the violent inclination, would have us give way to falsehood and act in selfish ambition, seeking our own glory and power and dominion, rather than the glory and dominion of El Elyon. Therefore, to live in submission to the Gospel of Truth, the evil inclination must be restrained, disciplined, and brought into the service of the good inclination, which is the love of Christ in us.

In the body and the vital (nefesh) there is no cutting off of the evil inclination (sitra ahara), the desire to receive; however, rather than the desire to receive for self alone, the desire to receive may be joined to the desire to give, the good inclination (sitra tov), and in service to the desire to give, the desire to receive is transformed and redeemed, for then the evil inclination is in submission to the dominion of the good inclination – the love of Christ, unconditional love.

If we ponder what it means to bring the evil inclination into the service of the good inclination we can study and contemplate the Sermon in the Mount in the Gospel of St. Matthew, for this is the thrust of the entire teaching that is given in it; likewise, we may meditate upon St. Paul's teaching in 1 Corinthians, where he speaks of the very essence of the Gospel of Truth and Christian life, explaining the single commandment of our Lord and Savior:

"Love one another as I have loved you."

The very essence of the Sermon on the Mount, and the very essence of love, is the desire to give – generosity and charity; it is concern for the welfare and well-being of others over and above one's own, and this is service to God, living in submission to God, for by rendering service to others, serving the people in Christ, serving all our relations in Christ, we actively serve the Holy One in life.

If we were to give thanks to God and praise God, worshipping God in spirit continually, but we did not serve the people and actively love one another, then our worship would have no meaning and would be in vain – for though worshiping in spirit we would not worship in truth.

Adonai Yeshua says to the Samaritan woman in the Gospel of St. John that the time is coming and is now here when we will no longer go to a manmade temple or to a special mountain top to worship God, but we will worship God in spirit and truth – in spirit, giving praise and thanks to God, and abiding in an unceasing communion of prayer in our heart, and in truth by active love and compassion, in acts of loving-kindness and service to the people, all our relations. This is true worship of El Elyon. Now as has been said, this belt of truth holds the Templar's sword at their side, and the sword of the Templar represents their action – seeking justice for the people and the land, and seeking mercy, bringing peace; through actions of loving-kindness in self-restraint we slay the evil inclination and manifest the good inclination, bringing the evil inclination into the service of the good, transforming the evil into good, uplifting evil as on the Holy Cross. In this way we shatter the husks of darkness – klippot, and uplift the holy sparks, all by way of the subjugation of the evil inclination in ourselves in service to the people and to God.

In the midst of our service, our duty to God, we do indeed "go out to holy war," but in truth we do not go out, but rather we go within, for the battlefield of the true holy war is in the human mind and heart where the demiurge and archons, and dark and hostile forces, seek their influence and dominion in the world in place of God, the True Light. As with the evil inclination in service to the good, the whole mind, heart and life of the Templar is brought into submission to God, to the Truth and Light revealed in Christ, so that while outwardly in service through action – through speech and deeds, inwardly our mind and heart is obedient to the Holy One, the exterior and interior life coexisting in harmony and peace; only then can we serve as Peacemakers bringing peace to the people and the land.

The belt of truth corresponds to Hod and Netzach, which is to say that it correspond the Divine Name of Yahweh Elohim Tzavaot, the Lord God of Hosts; and holding the sword on the side of the Templar, there is the implication of the sheath attached to this belt and the sword in its sheath – when there is complete submission to the Gospel of Truth, the Gospel of Peace, there is no need to draw the sword, but the angels of God will stand in defense of the faithful and elect.

As it well known to initiates of our Holy Order, drawing the sword and sheathing the sword is a theurgic action – the full power of Yahweh Elohim Tzavaot is in this, and the power of St. Michael and St. Uriel, and all of the luminous and enlightened ones from among the elohim and beni elohim. In submission to Christ and the Holy Spirit, when drawing the sword from its sheath it is not the Templar who draws the sword, but it is Christ and the Holy Spirit that takes up the action; thus, drawing the sword is not drawing the sword, but in all movements there is perfect repose – this is Truth, Amet.

In the midst of this there is a most subtle esoteric implication, for the sheath of the sword is as the body, and the sword within it is as the soul, and "drawing the sword" is the transference of consciousness from the material body to the body of light – the Solar Body of the Resurrection. This capacity is founded upon the sublimation and mastery of desire-energy, the Serpent Power uplifted and redeemed in the Holy Crown, the Star of the Divine I Am (Truth-Amet), and the belt of truth implies this self-mastery in Christ, this perfection of love, which is pure divine rapture, the Rainbow Body Attainment.

In this, perchance, with prayer and meditation, you may know the belt of truth so as to fasten it around your waist; it is inseparable from the holy sword of the Spirit, which is the Living Word of God.

The Knights Templar as Tzedek

The nature of righteousness is to enact the Truth and Light revealed in Christ, the Truth and Light revealed in our own experience – the Truth of Christ, Amet, is the basis of righteousness, or "doing what is right or just," and of the one who lives by their faith, who lives by the Truth and Light, as it is written in the scriptures, "It is accounted to them as righteousness."

Now, when we live in submission to God, naturally our desire is for God, our will is to do God's will; when our desire is God's desire, our will God's will, then God's Ratzon is our own – and that Ratzon is the Yesod-Foundation of our life, our guide and our purpose in all things.

The breastplate of a warrior is the shield of their torso – their heart and vital organs, and such is the nature of righteousness, actions in accord with the Truth and Light of Christ, the high priest of the Order of Melchizedek; in the midst of right action, in the midst of good works, when the Light of Christ shines from your heart, the love of Christ, the influence of archonic and demonic spirits cannot enter in and you will not error, you will not sin or miss the mark.

This is a world of action – an even if you do not take action, not acting is an action; under the law all actions generate karma, cause and effect, and so long as karma remains and the law is in effect, the soul remains in its bondage – the only way to true freedom is the cessation of the doer, as we behold in the Christ-bearer on the Holy Cross, the complete suspension of the doer, and with the suspension of the doer, the suspension of the law. It is then that the fullness of Divine Grace takes up our person and life, as we behold in Hayyah Yeshua, the Risen Messiah.
This is true righteousness – the cessation of the doer.
At the outset, of course, bound up in self-grasping, we are the doer; therefore in wisdom, as the doer, we do for the Lord, we serve the Lord in all things, assuming the view of a servant of

Christ and God, a slave of Christ. Then, perchance, with some spiritual maturation and the relaxation of the doer, making ourselves the instrument of Christ, setting ourselves into the hands of God, more and more it is the Holy One that moves us, and becoming emissaries and messengers of the Holy One, conscious agents of Christ and God, more and more it is Christ and the Holy Spirit that act with, in and through us, Christ and the Holy Spirit becoming the doer of everything, accomplishing everything. In fruition the doer abides in perfect repose – cessation, and there is rapturous union, Christ and the Holy Spirit becoming manifest as the holy man or holy woman, the Christ-bearer (Grail).

So long as there is a doer we will serve the Lord, Adonai; but in our service to the Lord we will seek the cessation of the doer, and this cessation is the perfection of service, the perfection of good works – all works being accomplished by Divine Grace.
Now, in the tradition the adepts and the masters are called tzaddik, which means "righteous one," but this term is not isolate to holy apostles – all of the faithful and elect are to be tzaddikim, all are to be the holy tzaddik, taking up their call and labor as a tzaddik; every true initiate shares in the spiritual labor of the holy tzaddik, the harvest of souls, each according to their gifts and their call in the Mother Spirit. There is no hierarchy implied by this term in the tradition, for all who live in Christ, all who live according to the Truth and Light revealed in Christ, are tzaddik – a righteous one.

There is an open secret in all of this, however, for in blood and flesh no one is tzaddik – the true Holy Tzaddik is the Light-presence (Christ) and Light-power (Holy Spirit) in us, the tzaddik being a person who lives in active and dynamic surrender to Christ and the Holy Spirit, Christ and the Holy Spirit taking up their person and life. Thus, it is taught by the masters of the tradition that in the experience of the inmost gradation of the Gnostic and Light Transmission, the Light-presence and Light-power of the outer tzaddik and the Light-presence and Light-power of the inner tzaddik are recognized as one and the same Christ Presence, and in that Holy Light the master and the disciple vanish, there is only Christ and the Holy Spirit, this Supernal Light-presence and Light-power.

In this we are speaking of the perfection of devekut – cleaving to Christ and the Holy Spirit, and of cleaving to El Elyon in Christ and the Holy Spirit; perfect devekut is rapturous union, the journey of the resurrection and ascension into the repose of union and enthronement – our union with Christ in God, the True Light. Now it must be said that this is an attainment that is *no attainment*, for first, this attainment is accomplished by Divine Grace, and by Divine Grace alone, so that in attainment we have attained nothing, but Christ and the Holy Spirit have attained victory with, in and through us; but more profoundly, however, this innate union with the source of our being, the union of our soul with Christ in God, is the very truth of our being – a truth that was, is and forever shall be, any apparent separation being completely illusory. Thus, there is nothing to attain, as though we lack something, but our "attainment" is the recognition and realization of a present truth of our soul in Christ, the Sacred Unity underlying all – it is our reintegration with the Pleroma of Light, as we behold in the ascension of the Risen Messiah.

When the doer is brought into cessation this reintegration is natural and spontaneous – Pure Divine Grace, Supernal Mercy (Tzedek).

When Christ and the Holy Spirit put the Blessed Name on you, then truly you will wear the Body of Vision, for Christ and the Holy Spirit will wear you – this is perfect righteousness.

We will pray:
Adonai have mercy on us, Messiah have mercy on us, Adonai have mercy on us; Arising to stand in Christ, We shall recline with Christ – Amen.

The Templar Shoes

We cannot proclaim the Gospel of Peace (Salem, Shalom) without first being established in the Holy Gospel, and we cannot bring peace unless we ourselves have the peace of Christ in us. Thus, these shoes for our feet that prepare us to proclaim the Gospel of Peace are our spiritual life and practice; specifically, it is the cultivation of a continuum of daily spiritual practice through which our interior life unfolds and we are empowered to active love and compassion.

Receiving teachings, we reflect upon them, contemplate them, meditate on them, and labor to integrate them into our lives; likewise, we study and contemplate the Holy Scriptures, seeking to increase our knowledge, understanding and wisdom, and we pray, meditate and perform sacred ceremony – we actively worship God and entertain good company, spiritual fellowship. With all of this, we remember and keep the Shabbat holy, and celebrate Shabbat.

The aim of all of this is the generation of the Sacred Heart, and self-realization in Christ – the Sacred Heart and our realization being the foundation of proclaiming the Gospel of Peace. Essentially, we will do whatever it takes for the generation of the Sacred Heart and process of our self-realization in Christ – we will take up whatever practices are necessary, apply whatever self-discipline is called for, and enact all spiritual works we are called to do by the Holy Spirit.

As shoes imply, we must be in the spiritual journey, the Path of the Great Ascension, and when we proclaim the Holy Gospel, we must speak from direct spiritual and mystical experience of the Risen Christ, speaking from faith and gnosis – when the Holy Gospel is our experience, then we have the proper foundation to proclaim it. We will speak of what we have seen and heard and know, and in such speech there is light-power, something of the Gnostic and Light Transmission.

Now there is something more subtle within and behind what St. Paul is saying, for when we are called to preach or to teach the Holy Gospel, or we are called to facilitate or lead any sacred event, always there is a spiritual work to be done beforehand, preparing the sacred space and laboring for the removal of obstructions in those who will attend. Thus, in one way or another, we purify and consecrate the sacred space, prepare ourselves, and pray for the people who are coming, as well as for all beings. Therefore, St. Paul is also speaking of the spiritual continuum in preparation for any sacred event – a continuum that begins well before any event, of which the event is the culmination.

Templars work very closely with lineage-holders in the tradition, and as much as lineage holders tend a spiritual continuum before sacred events, so also do the Templar initiates working with them – based upon their continuum Templars take up the sacred duty of purifying and consecrate sacred space before an event, clearing it of any shades or shadows, and calling upon Ha-Shem and the Shekinah to bless the sacred space and make it holy; then, throughout the event they serve as guardians of that sacred space and the people, ensuring that no klippotic influences enter into it. In the tradition, when we are called to speak, to preach or teach, we prepare no sermon or speech, but rather, we take up a continuum of prayer, contemplation and meditation, and we become open and sensitive to the Holy Spirit, and when it is time for us to speak we let the Mother Spirit speak with, in and through us, just as Yeshua Messiah taught us to do. This is our way in proclaiming the Holy Gospel or imparting teachings, it is in the power of the moment and in the Spirit – this, of course, assumes a well founded spiritual life and practice, and the experience of rebirth in the Mother Spirit.

Thus, we may understand preparation to proclaim the Gospel of Peace as whatever it takes to bring about our rebirth in the Mother Spirit, and whatever it takes to be completely open and sensitive to the Mother Spirit – whatever the Holy Spirit may call us to do.

Now something must be said of the term St. Paul uses for the Holy Gospel, the "Gospel of Peace." Having put on the belt of truth and breastplate of righteousness, as shoes for our feet we are to do whatever it takes to prepare us to proclaim the Gospel of Peace – truth is the knowledge of Christ Melchizedek, and the very name of Melchizedek literally means "king of righteousness," and he is called King of Salem, which means "king of peace." On an inner and secret level this alludes to the Gospel of Melchizedek – the inmost secret teachings of the Holy Gospel known to initiates of the tradition. Thus, on one level, these shoes are the recognition of the non-dual truth and the self-liberation of all that arises, just as it arises, in this recognition – hence, primordial contemplation as taught in the Melchizedek Transmission.

In closing we cannot help but mention the connection between these shoes and the Shoe Angel of Malkut, Sandalfon – the angel who is said to uplift the prayers of the faithful and elect to God. This invokes the admonition given to initiates during the Threefold Rite: "Enflame yourself with prayer – pray without ceasing; invoke often!" This, indeed, it what it means to put on these holy shoes, for in so doing we serve as an interface between heaven and earth, akin to shoes that are an interface between our body and the road we walk.

*With the mention of road, another aspect of these shoes, as known to initiates of the Order , is knowledge of the direction we are walking and calling upon the corresponding Divine Powers when we take up a spiritual labor in that direction.

In this, perhaps, you will know and understand how to put on these holy shoes and be prepared to proclaim the Holy Gospel of Christ.

The Templar Sword -explanation

St. John begins his gospel, teaching us, "In the beginning was the Word, and the Word was with God, and the Word was God. He was in the beginning with God. All things came into being through him, and without him not one thing came into being. What has come into being in him was life, and the life was the light of all people. The light shines in the darkness, and the darkness did not overcome it" (1:1-5).

According to St. Paul, the sword of the Spirit, the power of the Spirit, is the Word of God, Christ, the emanation of God, the True Light; the sword of the Templar is this Light-presence and Light-power, this flashing fire, which is the tongue of the Great Angel of Christ speaking to the seven holy churches in the Book of the Apocalypse – drawing the sword from its sheath this Divine Light flashes forth, dispelling all shades and shadows, and illuminating the world.

We shall say to all initiates of our Holy Order: Know yourself in Christ, and know the power of the Holy Sword that is in your hand – it is the power of the Blessed Name and Holy Spirit, the power of the Living Word of El Elyon, God Most High.
When you were dubbed, you bent your knee and bowed your head in honor of the image and likeness of the Human One, who is the image and likeness of Yahweh Elohim; for it is written, "Before the Blessed Name of Yeshua Messiah every head shall bow and every knee shall bend," and to the Blessed Name, "every spirit is subject," and so it is to the Holy Sword of the Spirit, the Living Word of El.

Consider the Name of Israel, the name of the spiritual elect, which means "one who rules as El," and so it is with the sword of the Spirit that God, the True Light, has placed into your hand, so that bending your knee and bowing yourself down you are uplifted in the Risen Christ to stand as a righteous warrior, a warrior of peace; and so as Melchizedek blessed Abram upon his return from battle with the Kings of Edom, so also are your blessed in Christ:

"Blessed are you by El Elyon, creator of heaven and earth; and blessed is El Elyon, who has delivered your enemies into your hand."

This is the blessing of the divine power of the First Commandment, the emanation of God, the True Light, which fulfilled is Christ, the Living Word: "I am Yahweh your El, who brought you out of the land of Egypt, out of the house of slavery; you shall not place the gods of others before me." This is the power of the Word of God that has been placed upon your tongue, the power of the sword of Spirit that has been placed in your hand – the power of Mercy and Judgment, the power to illuminate and liberate, the power of Compassion that brings Shalom (peace). Hallelu Yah! Praise the Lord!

Now a sword is Zain, which is also the number seven, the number of spiritual illumination and fruition; as is know to Christian Mekubalim, the sword of the Spirit is the power of the seven Sefirot of Construction, which emanate from Imma, the Holy Mother, the Word that Abba, the Father, has spoken in her. Here we may share a secret concerning the Holy Sword of the Spirit – it is the power of Yah (15), which is the power of two Zain (7) plus Alef (1); this power manifest in Mercy and Judgment, which are united in Compassion, and which is reflected by the two edges of the blade that are joined in a single point; and we shall say: Yod is the hand, and He is the sword in the hand. Let those who have ears, listen and hear, and understand!

The power of the seven Sefirot of Construction are manifest in the seven interior stars that shine in our Body of Light in Christ – the transcendental star above our head corresponding to the Supernals, specifically, to Habad (Binah-Hokmah-Da'at); receiving the Divine Light from above, the Mother's Force, these interior stars are made to shine from top to bottom, rightly ordered, and the Serpent Power is uplifted through them and redeemed in the Holy Crown, the Divine I Am – the Solar Body of the Resurrection comes into being in this way, the Divine Gnosis of the Risen Messiah.

This is the power of the sword of the Spirit in your hand!
Here we shall remind of the two swords – two Zain, spoken of
in the Gospel of St. Luke as previously quoted, for here we have
revealed the deeper esoteric mysteries of these two swords, two
Zain.

When you cleave to the Risen Messiah and Shekinah of Messiah,
through Divine Grace, the seven interior stars and seven Sefirot
of Construction are unified, and your soul is drawn up in ascent
into the Supernal Abode, Habad becoming embodied in you as
in Adonai Yeshua, Adonai Messiah – this is the Great Natural
Perfection which we call Christ Melchizedek (or
Messiah Melchizedek).

This is the power of the sword of the Spirit in your hand – it is the
power of Divine Rapture, Supernal Grace!
In this, perchance, you may know and understand the
wonderworking power in the Holy Sword, and know and
understand how drawing and sheathing the sword alone is a
great theurgic action, illuminating and liberating living spirits and
souls; when you know and understand how to draw the sword
of the Spirit from its sheath, then truly you will be a Peacemaker,
and you will stand among the Living Ones, the Immortals, on the
Day of Be-With-Us.

*If you wish to acquire deeper insight into this holy mystery,
contemplate Psalm 110, recognizing the truth of Yahweh and
realizing Adonai in you.

As we have said in our discourse: Your body is as the sheath
and your soul in Christ is as the sword – it is the Word of God;
transferring your soul into the Body of Light, in union with the
Risen Messiah, through Divine Grace your soul shall pass into the
Pleroma of Light, Eternal Life – this is the perfection of drawing
the sword from its sheath.

So we shall pray: Let our sword be drawn from its sheath by
Christ on the Day of Judgment in the End-Of-Days, amen!

Now, with the revelation of deep and esoteric mysteries concerning the sword of the Spirit, you must also know and understand the simple interpretation – this is your tongue confessing Yeshua is the Messiah, the Sun of El Elyon, and proclaiming the Holy Gospel in the boldness of true faith without shame or fear, laboring actively in the harvest of souls, seeking to bring souls to Christ, this Sanctuary of Grace that is the salvation of all. Having faith in our Lord and Savior, Yeshua Messiah, and having knowledge of the Good News, how could it be that we do not openly proclaim the Gospel of Peace, the Gospel of Truth? Indeed! The salvation of souls is at stake – how can we hold our tongues when the Holy Spirit calls us to speak?

In this you have full knowledge and understanding of the armor of God so as to put it on and stand firm – standing in Christ and God, the True Light.

Stand, therefore, and put on the whole armor of God, praying in the Spirit at all times in every prayer and supplication – to that end, keep alert and always persevere in supplication for all saints, for all tzaddikim.

In closing we can share another attribute of these aspects of the armor of God – in one teaching, as they are six, and correspond to Vau, they are attributed to the Sefirot of Zer Anpin un union with Nukva in the following way: The helmet to Hesed; the sword to Gevurah, the breastplate to Tiferet; the belt to Netzach and Hod; the shoes to Yesod; and the shield to Malkut. An entire set of teachings may be drawn from these correspondences – ask of the Holy Spirit and she will instruct and illuminate you.

Templar use of the armor

When there is a need to be strong in the Lord and to draw upon the strength of his power, anywhere, anytime, you can put on the whole armor of God and stand firm.

Envision luminous belt of truth around your waist, and a luminous breast plate of white brilliance with the insignia of our Holy Order in ruby red light upon it; and envision shoes of light and a shield of fiery light, and a helmet of light, and a sword of flashing fire in your hands – the armor of God is light and your body is light, the Spiritual Sun shining within you; as you envision this, remember the Blessed Name of Yeshua Messiah and call upon the Lord to give you strength. If you are in need of greater strength, then ask the Lord to send St. Michael and his hosts, and if you are in peril the great angel of the Lord and his host will deliver you, and so also anyone else who may be in need.

This is a simple practice of putting on the armor of God taught in our Holy Order.

When there is a person in need of strength or spiritual defense, but they are at a distance and you cannot go to them in the world, go to them in the spirit – send your angel to them.. Gather your consciousness as the Spiritual Sun in your heart and arise in your Body of Light, envisioning that you are wearing the armor of God, adorned akin to St. Michael; with conscious intention, go to the subtle atmosphere of the place where this person is, and as the Holy Spirit leads you, banish all shades and shadows, and bless the person with the Light of the True Cross. If they are in need of greater divine protection, call upon Ha-Shem to send St. Michael and his hosts, and pray that a ban of forty holy angels of St. Michael's hosts stand watch over them; if the need for divine protection is extreme and the person is in threat of their life and soul, then call upon Ha-Shem and ask him to send Kamael and his contingency of serafim.

If you wish to purify and consecrate sacred space, with sword in one hand and the Holy Bible in the other, invoke St. Michael and his hosts, and banish all shades and shadows with the sword and preach the word to all living spirits and souls with the Holy Bible – banishing all unclean and evil spirits, preach the Gospel of Peace, extending the Light of the True Cross into limitless space in all directions. As you receive spirits and souls in Christ, pray for their baptism in the Holy Spirit and their reception of the Supernal Chrism, and when next you partake of the Wedding Feast remember them and confirm their reception in Christ. Now, as known to Knights Commanders – adepts of our Holy Order, and to holy priests among Templars, this is a way to oath-bind archonic and demonic forces to service of the Light Transmission as wrathful guardians, setting them upon the path to their salvation. Touching the Holy Bible the spirit will speak the Blessed Name of Yeshua Messiah and confess, "Yeshua is Adonai," and they will speak the vow given to them to serve the Continuum of Light Transmission and to guard the faithful and elect, and they will be blessed in the Name of Adonai Yeshua Messiah and received into service, receiving their charge of holy orders – in fruition a Wedding Feast is celebrated, sealing the covenant before Ha-Shem.

*Of this practice of oath-binding we shall say it is an effective way to subjugate negative thoughts and emotions within one's own mind and heart.

Templar power prayer

At the outset of our discourse on the armor of God we gave the attributes of the various aspects of the armor to the Divine Names, the Sefirot of Atzilut; per the order of putting on the armor as St. Paul teaches it, this provides us with an order of prayer-invocation, the unification of our soul with the Holy Sefirot. Thus, calling upon the Divine Names corresponding to the various aspects of the armor of God, and taking up corresponding prayers to the attributes of the Holy Sefirot, unifying the soul with the Sefirot in this way, is a practice of putting on the whole armor of God.

In the seventh cycle of this discourse, sharing the mysteries of the sword of Spirit, the word of God, another attribute of the aspects of the armor was given, one corresponding to the union of Zer Anpin and Nukva – this becomes a specific cycle of prayers-invocations among Templar initiates that is called "auspicious circumstances in the bridal chamber."

The order of the Names of God in this teaching of attributes is as follows:
Yahweh Elohim Tzavaot
Yahweh Elohenu (or Yeshua Messiah)
Shaddai Adonai El
Elohim (or Elohim Givor)

Practice

Arising in the Body of Light according to the image of your Supernal Zelem, or the image of your Holy Maggid, the chant of Yahweh Elohim Tzavaot is taken up, with the conscious intention of the invocation of supernal and heavenly hosts into the psychic atmosphere of the earth, holy angels of God driving out darkness from the people and the land, and standing in guardianship of the assembly of the faithful and elect – a conscious intention for auspicious circumstances in the Continuum of Light

Transmission, the Order of the Holy Grail.

Then, magically transform your Body of Light into the image of the Risen Messiah and chant Yahweh Elohenu, holding the conscious intention of all spiritual forces subject to the Blessed Name and the intention of the tikkune and illumination of all living spirits and souls, all beings.

As you take up the chant of Shaddai, envision that you, in your Body of Light, transform into the image of the Great Angel of the Messiah speaking to the seven churches in the Apocalypse, and as you chant hold the conscious intention of opening the way for the Divine Revelation and the Great Ascension.

Then, envision that your Body of Light is transformed yet again, this time appearing as the image of the Woman of Light with the wings of the Great Eagle, and chanting Adonai hold the conscious intention of receiving souls into the Sanctuary of Grace and gathering all sparks into the Mystical Body of the Risen Messiah. When you take up the chant of El, become as the Holy Bride in the fullness of her power and glory in your Body of Light, and hold the conscious intention of mercy, blessings and grace poured out upon the faithful and elect, and all people in the land – the abundant blessings of the Spiritual Sun shining upon one and all alike.

In fruition, as you take up the chant of Elohim, magically transform into Archangel Michael, and envisioning yourself in the midst of the great hosts of the armies of God, hold the conscious intention of all that would distort, pervert, hinder or obstruct the flow of blessing and Light Transmission being removed from the assembly of the faithful and elect, as well as from the people and the land.

In conclusion, returning to the glory of your Supernal Zelem in Christ, and calling upon the Divine Names of El Elyon, Eheieh, Yah and Yahweh Elohim, hold the conscious intention of the greater advent of the Supernal Influx in the world, the full reception of the Holy Bride, the Second Coming of Christ – pray

147

for the swift coming of the Apocalypse.

Then, when all is accomplished, perhaps you will wish to celebrate a Wedding Feast to seal this theurgic action, but whether a Wedding Feast is performed or not, pray for the extension of the Light of the Messiah into all realms, worlds and universes of the Entirety, and pray that the blessings of this spiritual practice go to all sentient beings; let the Supreme Name of Adonai Yeshua Messiah be chanted with the conscious intention of proclaiming the Gospel of Peace, thus completing the theurgic movement.

*Each of these cycles of the prayer-invocation can be done purely with chants of the Divine Names and conscious intention, but corresponding prayers may be coupled with these drawing out greater light-power and blessings by prolonging the practice and engaging in theurgic acts by way of speaking in the Spirit. **From this, perhaps, you may discern how the main teaching that has been given on attributes of the Divine Names to the aspects of the armor of God might be used in cycles of prayer- invocation in a similar way.

In this we may glean some insight into what it means to "pray in the Spirit at all times in every prayer and supplication" – for on the one hand, it means that we take up prayers of the heart inspired by the Holy Spirit, letting the Holy Spirit pray with, in and through us; but on the other hand, it is prayer with the full knowledge of the Name of God and how to unify our soul with the Holy Sefirot by way of the Name of God (the wisdom of the Baal Shem, the Master of the Name) – in this prayers have their full power and effect, and great wonders may transpire through our prayers, for they are Spirit-filled.

St. Paul teaches us specifically that we are to pray for all saints, all tzaddikim, all faithful and elect, for they are our central focus – hence, in the harvest of souls our focus is those souls that are ripe and mature for harvest, first and foremost, and then for all who are as yet upon the vine awaiting their ripening in the Light of the Spiritual Sun, all in due season. Thus, this is our principle focus –

our holy kavvanah.

In closing we can say that this practice, itself, is a teaching of our Holy Order, worthy of contemplation and meditation to look and see what you might see, and to listen and hear what you might hear in the Spirit; but then, that's true of all Gnostic practices, they are expressions of teachings and the self-realization in Christ that is the aim of the Gnostic Christian life.

Appendix I

Secret names of Metatron - Introduction

"Enoch lived sixty-five years and begot Methuselah. And Enoch walked with God after he begot Methuselah, for three hundred years; and he begot founders and generations. All the days of Enoch were thus three hundred and sixty-five years. Enoch walked with God, and then he disappeared, for God took him." (Genesis 5:21–24)

In this chapter of the Holy Torah, it is said of all others that they died—but concerning Enoch (the Initiate), the Holy Torah says: "God took him." Therefore, according to tradition, Enoch was taken in an ascension, in divine rapture, without experiencing death. And thus, the masters of the tradition have taught that when Enoch was taken, he was transformed into the Archangel Metatron, the greatest of all the holy archangels, the archangel who presides over all the holy angels of God—Metatron being the emanation of Kether at the level of Beriyah, which corresponds to Tipheret at the level of Atzilut.

Here, we can recall the promise of Gayyah Yeshua in the Gospel of Thomas: that if we understand the interpretation of his inner and secret teachings, we will not taste death. Among the holy archangels, it is Metatron who holds this knowledge of Divine Wisdom taught by the Messiah.

On the Great Tree of Life, Tipheret of Atzilut becomes Kether of Beriyah—Tipheret is the Christ-Center of the Tree of Life. Thus, Metatron has been called the Archangelic Emanation of the Messiah or the Christ. Sandalfon, the archangel of Malkut, is the feminine twin of Metatron, and in their union, they are called Hua (or IAO, also Yew in the Gnostic Scriptures).

In tradition, no single image is given for Archangel Metatron. According to the prophetic and apocalyptic books of Enoch that describe his ascension and transformation into archangelic form, over a hundred names are given for this archangel, each representing a different emanation or aspect of Metatron. Essentially, he is an Archangel of Diamonds, or a "Supernal Being," and like a great gemstone, he has many facets—many emanations.

According to the Holy Torah, Enoch lived sixty-five years before he conceived his first child with his wife. This is the numerical value for the words hekhal (palace) and Adonai. As taught in the Book of Hekhalot, a soul enters into ascension through the chambers of the Divine Palace by unifying the soul with Adonai, walking with Ha-Shem as Enoch walked with Ha-Shem, and by invoking Archangel Metatron—such as through the sacred chants and kavvanot (intentions) given in this holy book, which records the oral tradition. After living sixty-five years, Enoch lived another three hundred years—the numerical value of the Hebrew letter Shin, the letter of the Holy Shekinah, whose addition to the Great Name YHVH brings forth the blessed name Yeshua. In total, Enoch lived three hundred and sixty-five years—corresponding to the number of days in a solar year, signifying the passage of the sun through each of the twelve signs of the zodiac (mazalot), representing the archetypes of the One Human, the fullness of the True Human Being.

As a human soul taking on an archangelic form, Metatron is unlike any other archangel, possessing intimate knowledge of God that only an enlightened human being can acquire, and also the knowledge of the mysteries of God and creation, from the exalted vantage point of the holy angels of God. According to the master of tradition, he assumes this form out of compassion—to remain present in the Great Matrix until all spirits and souls are redeemed, and to labor for the advent of the Supernal or Messianic Consciousness in all realms, worlds, and universes of the Great Matrix. Hence, all his innumerable light-emanations. Just as the legends of Enoch's ascension and his transformation into the Archangel Metatron suggest, Metatron is preeminently the archangel possessing knowledge of all forms of ascension, and is the first guide and guardian of the soul on the path of the Great Ascension among the maggidim (divine teachers). Naturally, therefore, those in the Christian stream who are called to be vision-bearers or prophets seek intimate knowledge of Metatron, invoking this great angel of God in his various forms for knowledge, conversation, and communion.

A sacred chant for Metatron taught within the Order was given in the Book of Hekhalot, but many other chants and many other names are taught in the tradition. With some knowledge of the names and how to invoke them, initiates of the Holy Order are empowered to call upon the various forms of Metatron to gain direct knowledge of this holy and divine being, and to draw blessings from this Prince of the Face.

If one wishes to call upon Archangel Metatron, let them first purify themselves, and walk in beauty and holiness, living according to the Holy Torah and the Holy Gospels. There is no true knowledge or communion with Archangel Metatron apart from this, for this holy maggid comes only to those who resemble the Sun of God—the children of the race of Seth.

Secret Names of Metatron

Torahkiel Yahweh – This is the emanation of Metatron as Baal Shem, Master of the Name, and Master of the Torah and the Gospels. If an initiate seeks knowledge of the Divine Name, or seeks insight into the secret mysteries of the Torah and the Gospels, this is the emanation of the archangel they will invoke. It also corresponds to the knowledge of the 72 Names of God. (Chant: Torahkiel IAOWAY – "Yahweh" being pronounced only as vowel sounds; also Ta-Ra-Ha-Ki-El Yah-Ha-Va-Ha)

Zer Yahweh (Little Yahweh) – This is the emanation of Metatron manifested as the archangels and angelic orders of Zer Anpin. There are peaceful, wrathful, and joyful forms of this emanation. (Chant: Za-Ra Yo-Ho-Vo-Ho)

Sar Ha-Olam – This is the emanation of Metatron as the Dimension of Light within and behind creation—the manifestation of the Continuum of Luminous Transmission. (Chant: Sa-Ra O-La-Ah-Ma)

Na'ar – This is the emanation of Metatron with the knowledge of the end of days.
(Chant: Na-Ah-Ah-Ra)

Shaddai – This is the emanation of Metatron as the aspect of the Lord in dream visions. It is a wrathful emanation of judgment; initiates may invoke this emanation if they seek a dream vision or a movement of divine judgment.
Yoel – This is the emanation of Metatron that communicates the perfect joy or happiness of God, and leads to union and rapture with the Holy Shekinah.
(Chant: Yo-Ah-La)

Surya – This is the emanation of Metatron as the Holy Prince of the New Jerusalem. As suggested by the title "The Young Man," he appears as a beautiful youth of sixteen years, yet upholding the illumination of the Ancient of Days.
(Chant: Sur-Yah-Ha)

Yofiel – This is the emanation of Metatron that breaks through the klippot (shells) obstructing Divine Will and the Transmission of Light.
(Chant: Yo-Peh-Yah-Ah-Lo Peh-Peh-Peh)

Pisgon – This is the emanation of Metatron bearing the power of transformation.
Sitriel – This is the emanation of Metatron with the knowledge of Paradise and the secret understanding of the Garden of Eden.
(Chant: See-Ta-Ra-Yah-Al)

Tzahtzehiyah – This is the emanation of Metatron with knowledge of the cleaving to the Living Father, Abba.
(Chant: Tza-Tze-EE-Yah)

Zerahyahu – This is Metatron with the knowledge of the inner presence of God and of Divinity itself.
(Chant: Ze-Ra-Ha-Ya-Hu)

Taftefiah – This is the emanation of Metatron arising as a great and furious force against evil and darkness—binding and releasing.
(Chant: Ta-Peh-Te-Peh-Yah-Ah)

Hayyot – This is the emanation of Metatron as the order of angels over which he presides: the Hayyot Ha-Kodesh, or "Holy Living Creatures," representing Kether at the level of Yetzirah.
Hashesiyah – This is the joyful emanation of Metatron as an angel of the Holy Shekinah.
(Chant: Ha-Shay-Say-Yah)

Duvdeviyah – This is the emanation of Metatron that holds dominion over the mazalot (zodiac or destinies) according to the will of Ha-Shem—the dominion of fates and fortunes. An initiate seeking to shift the balance of fate or fortune will invoke this aspect of Metatron.
(Chant: Due-Day-Va-EE-Yah)

Yahsiyah – This is the emanation of Metatron that reveals the Supernal Light from above and below, and reveals the union of Mother and Daughter, Father and Son.
(Chant: Yah-See-Yah)

Palpeltiyah – This is the emanation of Metatron that sets things in motion and removes obstructions from the flow of events. (Chant: Pa-La-Peh-La-Yo-Yah-Ha)

Havhaviyah – This is the emanation of Metatron as an angel of the Holy Shekinah, granting blessings and teaching the wonders of sacred labor.
(Chant: Ha-Va-Ha-Va-Yo-Yah)

Haviyahu – This is the emanation of Metatron with the knowledge and understanding of the embodiment of the Supernal Shekinah.
(Chant: Ha-Vey-Yah-Hu)

Veruah – This is the emanation of Metatron as the Spirit of Vav; Metatron as the one who forms spiritual connections.
(Chant: Vey-Re-U-Ah)

Migirkon – This is Metatron as the great guardian of the Bridal Chamber.
Itmon – This is an emanation of Metatron in one of his strangest and other-dimensional forms, possessing knowledge of travel through hidden dimensions, as well as the understanding of meta-dimensional geometric forms underlying the Great Matrix.
(Chant: EE-Ta-Ma-On)

Batsran – This is the feminine emanation of Metatron as the Holy Angel of Nukva, the Daughter or Young Bride.
(Chant: Ba-Tza-Ron)

Tishbash – This is an emanation of Metatron with the knowledge and understanding of consecrations of great power.
(Chant: Ta-Yah-Sha-Ba-Sha)

Tishgash – This is an emanation of Metatron with the knowledge and understanding of the power of great purification. (Chant: Ta-Yah-Sha-Ga-Sha)

Mitspad – This is an emanation of Metatron that removes obstructions to the accomplishment of good works. (Chant: Mi-Tza-Pay-Ah-Da)

Midrash – This is Metatron as the revealer of secret events and hidden correspondences, and as the Keeper of Knowledge and Storyteller among the angels of God.
Matzmetziyah – This is the emanation of Metatron with the knowledge of the firmaments of Shamayim (Heaven) and how souls pass through these intervals.
(Chant: Ma-Tza-Me-Tzay-EE-Ya-Ha)

Patzpetziyah – This is the emanation of Metatron that purifies souls in their passage between the lower and upper dwelling places of Shamayim.
(Chant: Pa-Tza-Peh-Tzay-EE-Ya-Ha)

Zevtiyahu – This is the emanation of Metatron with the sword of righteousness in the inner presence of God; it is also the emanation of Metatron who walks with the highest-ranking holy tzaddikim—those of the Supernal Fulfillment.
(Chant: Zay-Vo-Te-Yah-Hu)

Miton – This is the emanation of Metatron with the knowledge of God within God.
Adrigon – This is a fearsome and awe-inspiring aspect of Metatron within the Inner Sanctuary of the Divine Order.
Ruach Piskonit – This is Metatron as the illumination of the Holy Princess, and also an emanation of Sandalfon.
Itatiyah – This is the emanation of Metatron with the knowledge of the magic and sorcery of the ancient races, including those of sub-gods and goddesses.

(Chant: Yah-Ta-Yah-Ya-Ho)

Tavtavel – This is the emanation of Metatron with the knowledge
of the mysteries of crucifixion and the dark nights of the soul;
thus also the understanding of the culmination point of all things
within the Great Matrix. Some have said that this is Metatron
with the consciousness of the goodness in all things.
(Chant: Tov-Tov-Al)

Hadraniel – This is the emanation of Metatron from the left, who
breaks the dominion of the klippot (husks/shells) and evildoers.
(Chant: Ha-Da-Ra-Nu-Yah-Al)

Tatriel – This is Metatron with the knowledge of the redemption
of the Serpent.
(Chant: Ta-Toe-Ra-EE-El)

Ozah – This is the emanation of Metatron that reveals the mystery
of the generation of light bodies, or the mystery of the vesture of
light worn by the ascending Messiah and the Righteous in their
ascent.
(Chant: O-Za-Ah-Ha)

Eved – This is a hidden emanation of Metatron.
Galiel – This is an emanation of Metatron as a great ofan (wheel-
being) who holds the knowledge of spirits in the intermediaries
that follow judgment.
(Chant: Ga-Al-Ya-Al)

Tzaftzefiel – This is an emanation of Metatron arising as the
champion of the tzaddikim (righteous ones).
(Chant: Tza-Peh-Tzey-Peh-EE-El)

Hatzpatziel – This is an emanation of Metatron as the watcher
of the gates of the Other Side, and it is an emanation that moves
across the Great Abyss.
(Chant: Ha-Tza-Peh-Ah-Tza-Yah-El)

Sagmagigrin – This is the emanation of Metatron with knowledge of the great powers of the universes that passed through the LORD before the creation of the current cosmic cycle.

Yefefiah – This is Metatron with the power to pierce insight, dispelling all falsehood and illusion.
(Chant: Ye-Peh-Eh-Peh-EE-Ah)

Estes – This is a hidden emanation of Metatron.

Safkas – This is the emanation of Metatron as the Great Kerub (Cherub) at the right of the Grand Gate, the Abyss.

Saftas – This is the emanation of Metatron as the Great Kerub at the left of the Grand Gate, the Abyss.

These emanations hold the knowledge of the mysteries of Da'at.

Mivon – This is Metatron who reveals the secret knowledge of God through the power of Vav.

Asasiah – This is Metatron with the secret knowledge of the emanation body of Melchizedek, inseparable from the Great Matrix.
(Chant: Ah-Sa-Ah-Sa-EE-Ah)

Avtzangosh – This is the emanation of Metatron that knows the wonders that transpire in God beyond God, in the Godhead.
(Chant: Ah-Vo-Tza-Nu-Go-Sha)

Margash – This is the emanation of Metatron subjugating and destroying the titanic forces, the giants, and the fallen ones.
Atropatos – This is Metatron bringing justice to sorcerers and false prophets.

Tzaftzefiyah – This is Metatron arising as the champion of the tzaddikim, but with the mitigation of judgment through grace.
(Chant: Tza-Peh-Tzay-Peh-EE-Yah)

Zerahiyah – This is Metatron with the knowledge of glory within glory, light within light, and the essence of light in Ain Sof.
(Chant: Zey-Eh-Ray-Hey-EE-Yo-Ah)

Tamtemiyah – This is the emanation of Metatron as the initiator among the holy angels of the Divine Order, holding knowledge of the power of the Great Partzufim and the immortals.
(Chant: Ta-Ma-Te-Me-EE-Yah)

Rasesiyah – This is the aspect of Metatron within the Council of the Stars, holding the knowledge of the Great Fire in the "Spine of the Dragon."
(Chant: Ra-Say-See-Yah)

Amisiyah – This is the emanation of Metatron with knowledge of secret covenants and wonders performed by the tzaddikim, and the knowledge of how they were accomplished.
(Chant: Ah-Me-See-Yah)

Hakham – This is the emanation of Metatron with knowledge of the wonders of working with the primal element of Spirit-Space.
(Chant: Ha-Ka-Ha-Ma)

Bibiyah – This is the emanation of Metatron with the knowledge and understanding of the spiritual forces that make up the Great Matrix, the higher and lower worlds; also, the emanation with knowledge of the Father in the Mother, and of her utterance of the Living Word.
(Chant: Ba-Yah-Ba-Yah-Yah)

Tzavtziyah – This is the emanation of Metatron with the knowledge and wisdom of ibur (soul impregnation), and the awareness of all iburim—the souls of the righteous, the faithful, and the elect who join together.
(Chant: Tza-Va-Tze-Yah)

Tzaltzeliyah – This is the emanation of Metatron with the secret knowledge of karmic connections in the exchange of sparks between souls, and how soul interactions facilitate their evolution; it also holds the knowledge of all incarnations of souls.

(Chant: Tza-La-Tze-Ley-Yah)

Kalkelmiyah – This is Metatron with the perfect knowledge of the law of cause and effect, and the effect of grace, and all that may transpire from it.
(Chant: Ka-La-Kay-Lay-Me-Yah)

Hoveh Hayah – This is Metatron as the emanation of the Great Angel of Hayyah Elohim, in pure mercy and grace, enlightening and liberating those who gaze steadfastly.
(Chant: Ho-Vo-Ho Ha-Yah-Ha)

Yahweh Vehayah – The meaning and power of this name is known to the initiates and may only be spoken to one who already knows; but here we can say it is the knowledge of "THAT-WHICH-IS-TRANSPIRING" within and behind what appears, and the awareness of the presence and glory of God permeating creation.
(Chant: IAOWAY Vey-Ha-Yah)

Tetrasiyah – This is the emanation of Metatron with the knowledge and understanding of the four Olamot (worlds), and also the mystery of the Father and Mother, Son and Daughter.
Uvayah – This is Metatron with the full power of the Supernal Vav and the soul of the Messiah.
(Chant: U-Va-Yah)

Shosoriyah – This is the emanation of Metatron with the knowledge of how to enchant the Holy Shekinah, bringing forth her joy.
(Chant: Sho-So-Ro-EE-Yah)

Vehofnehu – This is the emanation of Metatron with the knowledge of the primordial unity of origin and its shattering, and with the knowledge and understanding of the power of reunification/rectification (tikkune).
(Chant: Vey-Ho-Peh-Ney-Hu)

Yeshhayah – This is Metatron assuming the aspect of the emanation of the One Human of Light (the Messiah). (Chant: Ye-Sha-Ha-Yo-Ha)

Malmeliyah – This is Metatron with the knowledge and understanding of the development and evolution of life forms in their aspiration toward the Highest Life.
(Chant: Ma-La-Me-Ley-EE-Yah)

Gale Raziyah – This is the emanation of Metatron with the secret knowledge of the generation of heavens by the tzaddikim, and the knowledge of the Glory Body of Melchizedek.
(Chant: Ga-La-Eh Ra-Zee-Yah)

Atatiyah – This is Metatron with the knowledge of the Fire of the Chrism.
(Chant: Ah-Ta-Ah-Te-Yah)

Emekmiyahu – This is the emanation of Metatron supporting the fortune of those who know the Truth of God and become the image of that Embodied Divine Truth.
(Chant: Ah-Ma-Ka-Me-Yah-Hu)

Tzatzelim – This is Metatron as the image of Righteousness, possessing the knowledge of the Supernal images of all the righteous ones of all times—past, present, and future. (Chant: Tza-Ah-Zey-La-Yah-Ma)

Tzavniyah – This is Metatron with the knowledge of "the way of cessation" and self-liberation through the Great Natural Perfection.
(Chant: Tza-Va-Na-Yah-Yo-Ho)

Giatiyah – This is the emanation of Metatron with the knowledge of the heavens and all abodes within gilgulim (cycles of soul incarnation), and the knowledge of all spirits and souls in them, and how they enter and leave.
(Chant: Ge-Ah-Te-Yah)

Parshiyah – This is Metatron with the knowledge of the "concealments" that reveal.
(Chant: Pa-Ra-Sha-EE-Yah)

Shaftiyah – This is the emanation of Metatron who goes forth and returns to labor for the return of the Holy Bride from her exile. It is a fierce emanation that casts down her enemies.
(Chant: Sha-Peh-Tey-Yah)

Hasmiyah – This is Metatron with the knowledge of the Body of Truth of Melchizedek.
(Chant: Ha-Sa-Ma-EE-Yah)

Sharshiyah – This is the emanation of Metatron in the Solar Body of consuming fire, self-made of fire.
(Chant: Sha-Ra-She-Yah)

Geviriyah – This is the emanation of Metatron as a great angel of pure force and fire, the force of the universe's apocalypse, the dissolution of all.
(Chant: Ge-Vey-Rey-Yah)

Metatron – This is the name and emanation of the Initiate who attains union with Elyon, and it is the name of the power of all emanations of the Great Maggid of El Elyon, the Most High God.
(Chant: Ma-Ta-Ra-Oh-Na)

The chants given reflect the energetic quality of the emanations rather than the literal pronunciation of the names.

How to Invoke the Names of Metatron
When the navi (seer/prophet) seeks to invoke the emanations of the Supernal Maggid, they will undergo a continuum of purification, and through prayer and meditation they will praise and bless Ha-Shem. They will unify their soul with the Holy Sefirot, the Divine Names; only when this unification is accomplished will they invoke the emanations of the Supernal Maggid, because apart from this unification, invoking the Great Maggid is judgment.

The names/emanations of Metatron are invoked within a Holy Sanctuary or Sacred Circle, and they are often invoked through the Wheel of Light—the invocations of the Supernal Maggid represent one of the dimensions of the secret consecration of the Wheel of Light in the tradition.

At times, when there is a vision needed for the people, the one who sees will enter a spiritual retreat, and the invocations of the Great Maggid will become their sole focus, until the heavens open, the vision is born, and the voice of Yahweh comes to give a word for the people.

The crystal skull is a common talisman of the Archangel Metatron, and the sacred feathers of the eagle—as well as the vulture—are associated with Metatron, especially those of the eagle.

Typically, before seeking the circle of knowledge with the Supernal Maggid, initiates will seek knowledge and conversation with the Archangels of the Sacred Circle, and the other Archangels of the Tree of Life. Likewise, they will call upon the emanations of Metatron in their daily continuum only when they have received the knowledge and permission from divine authority to do so—until that moment, they always perform a special continuum to invoke the Supernal Maggid, ensuring that they are prepared to receive the spiritual influx that comes with the Archangel Metatron.

Made in the USA
Monee, IL
29 April 2025

16628116R00095